Welcome,

If you're reading this, you're likely a nurse or nurse practitioner craving something more autonomy, more income, and more impact. Maybe you're drawn to aesthetics but overwhelmed by the noise. Maybe you've seen the filtered Instagram reels, the "six-figure in six weeks" promises, but what you really want is a roadmap grounded in science, strategy, and service.

You're in the right place.

This guide was created for aspiring and practicing nurse practitioners who want to enter aesthetics with integrity, clinically sound, culturally competent, and business-savvy. It's not just about getting certified or picking the right toxin. It's about understanding the bigger picture: the anatomy, the ethics, the economics, and the empowerment that come with building something of your own.

MAHOGANY DERMATOLOGY
NURSING | EDUCATION | RESEARCH™

Our mission is to bridge the gap in dermatology and aesthetics education, with an emphasis on skin of color, business acumen, and digital fluency. Founded by a nurse practitioner, for nurse practitioners, we equip you with the tools to live the life you worked so hard for. This is your invitation to enter the field with clarity and confidence, not confusion and burnout.

Let's redefine what success looks like, for you, your clients, and the future of our profession.

Dr. Kimberly Madison, DNP

TABLE OF CONTENTS

Foundation & Future of Aesthetics

1. What Is Aesthetics?
2. A Brief History of the Aesthetic Medicine Industry
3. Where the Industry Is Headed: Future Trends
4. Artificial Intelligence in Aesthetics: Opportunity or Threat?

Scope, Training & Clinical Readinessmm

5. Who Can Practice Aesthetics? Know Your Scope
6. Clinical Training - Evaluating Legitimacy
7. Questions to Ask During Hands-On Training
8. Understanding Race and Ethnicity in Aesthetic Care
9. Cultural Considerations in Beauty and Aging
10. Anatomy and Physiology for Aesthetic Nurse Practitioners
11. Patient Evaluation: Laying the Clinical Foundation

Heritage, Identity, & Influence

12. Aesthetic Preferences in Melanated Skin
13. Aging in Skin of Color
14. Perceptions of Beauty: Black, Latin, East & South Asian, Middle Eastern, and White Beauty Ideals
15. Social Media & The Nurse Practitioner's Role in Shaping Beauty Norms

TABLE OF CONTENTS

Clinical Conditions in Aesthetic Practice

16. Skin Texture Concerns
17. Dermatosis Papulosa Nigra
18. Acne and Postinflammatory Hyperpigmentation (PIH)
19. Melasma: Pathophysiology and Management
20. Alopecia and Scalp Concerns
21. Hair Removal in Skin of Color
22. Hypertrophic Scars and Keloids
23. Periorbital Rejuvenation

Treatment Modalities & Techniques

24. Facial Rejuvenation and Contouring
25. Neuromodulators: Botox & Beyond
26. Soft Tissue Augmentation (Fillers)
27. Laser and Light-Based Devices in Diverse Skin Tones
28. Surgical Treatment Options
29. Topical Treatments for Aesthetic Conditions

Business, Research & Education

30. Navigating Patient Care & Building the Business
31. DNP vs PhD: What's the Difference & Do You Need It?
32. DNP Project Ideas in Aesthetics
33. Opportunities for PhD Nurse Scientists
34. Skin of Color in Aesthetic Practice
35. Gaps in Education, Research, and Clinical Training

TABLE OF CONTENTS

36. What's Missing in Marketing: The Cultural Disconnect

37. The Pros and Cons of the Aesthetic Industry

Legal, Financial, & Professional Growth

38. Business Mentors and Legal Experts You'll Need

39. Finance, Liability, and Practice Protection

40. Resources for Ongoing Learning

41. ChatGPT Prompts, Worksheets & Clinical Templates

42. Launch Your Skincare Line

43. Beyond Skincare: 20 Innovative Business Ideas

BONUS: Market Analysis & Business Growth

44. Business Ideation to Creation

45. Market Analysis & Projected Profits

46. SWOT Analysis

47. Business Growth Strategy to Become a CEO

48. AI Chief Financial Officer

49. Top 20 Questions from Aspiring and Experienced Aesthetic NPs

50. How to Connect with Me

Appendix

51. You're Hired! 60-90 Day Onboarding & Training Plan

52. 4-Week Botox Training Roadmap for a New Aesthetic NP

53. 4-Week Filler Training Roadmap for a New Aesthetic NP

54. Botox & Filler Pricing Calculator

55. Sample Adverse Event SOP for an NP-Led Medical Spa

TABLE OF CONTENTS

56. SOP Starter Kit for NP-Led Aesthetic Practices

PART I: LAYING THE FOUNDATION

- **What Is Aesthetics?**
    - A foundational overview of the aesthetic medicine field, what it is, what it isn't, and why it's a growing opportunity for Nurse Practitioners seeking more freedom, flexibility, and financial reward.

- **A Brief History of the Aesthetic Medicine Industry**
    - This chapter explores the evolution of aesthetic medicine, how it moved from an elite luxury to a more accessible service, and the role nurses are increasingly playing in this transformation.

- **Where the Industry Is Headed: Future Trends**
    - From regenerative medicine to virtual consultations, we explore emerging trends that every NP entering aesthetics should be aware of to future-proof their practice.

- **Artificial Intelligence in Aesthetics: Opportunity or Threat?**
    - A candid look at the rise of AI, its current applications in aesthetics, and how NPs can leverage this technology ethically and effectively.

Chapter 1: What Is Aesthetics?

Aesthetic medicine is more than Botox and beauty trends, it's a transformative, patient-centered specialty that merges science, art, and wellness to help individuals look and feel their best. For nurse practitioners (NPs), it represents an exciting frontier of clinical practice that offers autonomy, creativity, and the opportunity to build a business on your own terms.

At its core, aesthetic medicine focuses on elective procedures that enhance physical appearance, improve skin health, and support self-confidence. These treatments can include neuromodulators, dermal fillers, chemical peels, laser therapies, microneedling, hair restoration, and more. But unlike traditional medical care, aesthetics is rarely about addressing disease; it's about refining the patient's relationship with their image, their aging process, and their definition of beauty.

Aesthetic care can be both deeply personal and deeply powerful. It invites NPs to combine our clinical expertise with emotional intelligence, cultural awareness, and an understanding of visual harmony. This is not vanity work, it's wellness work. When delivered ethically and skillfully, aesthetic treatments can improve mental health, enhance quality of life, and restore a sense of control and confidence for the patient.

That said, it's just as important to understand what aesthetics is not. It's not a quick-fix business. It's not "easy money." And it's certainly not immune to complications, liability, or ethical dilemmas. This is a field where your training, values, and critical thinking matter. Patients trust you with their face, and sometimes their identity. That responsibility should never be taken lightly.

So why are more NPs entering this field now? The answer is layered: flexibility, financial reward, and freedom from the constraints of traditional healthcare systems are all major drivers. Aesthetic practice allows NPs to carve out a niche that's aligned with our passions and lifestyle goals. Whether you want to open your own medical spa, collaborate with a plastic surgeon, or add aesthetic services to an existing wellness or primary care practice, the options are as expansive as your vision.

As you move through this book, you'll gain a realistic view of what it takes to succeed in aesthetics, not just clinically, but ethically, culturally, and entrepreneurially. Because entering this space is not just about mastering injectables, it's about mastering intention, identity, and influence in a rapidly evolving industry.

Chapter 2: A Brief History of the Aesthetic Medicine Industry

Before aesthetic nursing became a recognized specialty, before dermal fillers and lasers became routine in clinical practice, and before nurse practitioners launched their own cosmetic clinics, the relationship between medicine, beauty, and self-care had already been established across centuries and civilizations.

Many histories begin with ancient Egypt, and for good reason. The Egyptians practiced sophisticated forms of skincare and cosmetic enhancement using natural oils, clays, herbs, and minerals. Both men and women valued healthy skin and practiced daily rituals to protect and maintain it. Cleopatra remains a well-known figure for her reported use of milk baths and botanical treatments, but she represents just one chapter in a much broader African story.

Throughout the African continent, skin care and body care were part of daily life, community wellness, and cultural identity. In West Africa, shea butter was not a commercial product but a generational remedy used to soothe, moisturize, and protect the skin. In Namibia, Himba women developed and still use a red ochre and butterfat blend to shield their skin from sun and wind while also honoring aesthetic tradition. Moroccan women used argan oil, black soap, and rhassoul clay long before these became popular in Western skincare routines. These practices were not merely cosmetic. They were expressions of knowledge, resourcefulness, and care developed through lived experience and oral tradition.

This deep understanding of the body and the environment laid the foundation for many of the principles that still guide aesthetic practice today. Yet much of this legacy has been left out of formal histories. Instead, the timeline often picks up again in Europe during the Renaissance, where artistic ideals of beauty began to influence grooming, fashion, and early cosmetic formulations.

By the 19th and early 20th centuries, aesthetic treatments began to intersect more formally with medical practice. The first recorded cosmetic surgeries, facelifts, and injectable treatments were developed, and physicians began to explore appearance-related interventions as part of clinical care. Dermatology and plastic surgery grew in both complexity and popularity, creating opportunities for more professionals to participate in the evolving field.

In the 1990s, aesthetic nursing emerged as a distinct specialty. As non-invasive treatments became safer and more accessible, dermatologists and plastic surgeons began training nurses in procedures such as botulinum toxin injections, chemical peels, and dermal fillers. Nurses were uniquely positioned to deliver these services, combining clinical knowledge, patient-centered care, and procedural skill.

As patient demand increased, formal training and certification programs were developed. By the early 2000s, aesthetic nursing was recognized as a professional path requiring advanced knowledge of anatomy, skin conditions, and cosmetic science. Organizations like the American Society of Plastic Surgeons and the American Association of Aesthetic Medicine and Surgery helped define roles and create educational standards.

Today, nurse practitioners in aesthetic medicine are respected as clinical leaders and business owners. They provide high-quality, ethical care in medical spas, dermatology clinics, and private practices across the country. Their role extends beyond procedures to include consultation, education, follow-up care, and practice management.

The history of aesthetic nursing is still being written, but it is important to acknowledge its deeper roots. The use of natural products, intentional self-care, and skin health practices began long before formalized education and licensing. African traditions, often overlooked, were some of the earliest to integrate beauty and wellness with practical, body-focused care. These contributions are not a footnote. They are part of the foundation on which the modern aesthetic industry stands.

Shifts In Practice

Aesthetic medicine didn't start as the accessible, thriving field we know today. It began as a niche service for the wealthy, something reserved for red carpets, magazine covers, and high-society circles. Procedures were limited, expensive, and often invasive. There was little representation, little transparency, and even less regulation. But over time, everything changed.

The field has evolved from one centered on surgical intervention to one that now prioritizes non-invasive and minimally invasive treatments. As technology advanced and public interest grew, aesthetic medicine moved out of the shadows and into mainstream culture. Today, it's no longer just about turning back the clock, it's about choice, confidence, and preventative care.

We've also seen a shift in who delivers this care. Once dominated by plastic surgeons and dermatologists, the aesthetic space is now expanding to welcome nurse practitioners and other advanced practice providers. Our clinical expertise, holistic approach, and ability to build trust make us uniquely positioned to offer aesthetic services with both safety and sensitivity.

But let's be clear, our presence in this industry hasn't always been welcomed with open arms. We've had to push for seats at the table, demand high-quality training, and prove that we belong here. And we do.

We're part of a movement that's reshaping what aesthetic medicine looks like, and who it serves. More people of color. More diverse body types. More inclusive definitions of beauty. We're not just learning the techniques, we're redefining the culture.

By understanding where this industry came from, we can better appreciate the responsibility we carry as we move it forward. We're not here to replicate outdated beauty standards. We're here to offer something better: care that is ethical, inclusive, safe, and rooted in the patient's goals, not society's expectations.

The Evolving Role of Nurse Practitioners in Aesthetic Medicine
Historically, many doctors, especially those in traditional fields like internal medicine or surgery, did not want to be involved in aesthetics because it was often seen as more superficial or less medically significant compared to their other clinical specialties. Aesthetics was initially viewed as more of an elective service, with some practitioners considering it outside the scope of serious medical practice.

Nurse Practitioners, on the other hand, played a pivotal role in the early days of aesthetic medicine. Many NPs, particularly those with backgrounds in dermatology or plastic surgery, were at the forefront of performing aesthetic procedures like Botox injections, dermal fillers, and chemical peels. They were often the ones seeking out additional training and certifications to meet the growing demand for these services, as aesthetic procedures became more popular and accessible to a wider range of patients.

As the field expanded and the demand for aesthetic services grew, NPs became instrumental in establishing standardized training programs and frameworks for delivering these procedures safely and effectively. Over time, many NPs became leaders in the industry, offering both clinical expertise and business acumen in running successful aesthetic practices.

Recently, however, there has been a broader acceptance of aesthetics within the medical community, with more physicians, particularly those specializing in dermatology, plastic surgery, and even certain internal medicine fields, seeing the potential for career growth and revenue in aesthetic practices. This shift has led to a greater collaboration between NPs and physicians in aesthetics.

That being said, NPs remain highly sought after in the aesthetic industry due to our clinical skills, patient-centered care, and artistic approach to aesthetics, making us an essential part of the landscape.

Chapter 3: Where the Industry Is Headed: Future Trends

As nurse practitioners entering aesthetics, we aren't just stepping into an industry, we're stepping into a moment. One that's rapidly evolving, increasingly tech-driven, and shaped by changing cultural values. If we want to build practices that last, we need to go where the puck is going, not where it is right now.

The first major shift we're seeing is toward regenerative aesthetics. This isn't just about filling lines or freezing movement anymore. It's about supporting the body's natural ability to heal and renew. Treatments like PRF (Platelet-Rich Fibrin), stem cell therapies, and exosome technology are starting to replace older, surface-level solutions. Patients are asking for results that are subtle, sustainable, and rooted in wellness, and we're rising to meet that demand.

We're also watching the rise of virtual consultations and digital skincare ecosystems. What used to be limited to in-person visits is now happening over secure video, with digital analysis tools helping us assess skin health and treatment readiness. Teleaesthetics won't replace the in-person experience, but it's expanding access and letting us engage patients earlier in their care journey.

Inclusivity and representation are no longer optional; they're essential. Patients are seeking providers who understand their unique skin needs, cultural values, and aesthetic goals. As clinicians, we're embracing a more individualized approach to beauty, one that celebrates cultural richness instead of standardizing it. That's why providers with knowledge of skin of color, different aging patterns, and cultural beauty ideals are in higher demand than ever.

And then there's technology. Artificial intelligence, Augmented Reality (AR) filters, diagnostic imaging, and even robotic injectors are being tested in aesthetic settings. As NPs, we need to stay curious and critical. Not everything new is better, but when used wisely, tech can help us deliver safer, more personalized care. We'll talk more about that in the next chapter.

The aesthetic industry is also becoming more patient-led. People are walking into our offices educated, informed, and ready to ask questions. They want transparency, natural results, and providers who listen. We're no longer just offering services, we're building relationships and becoming partners in long-term confidence and self-expression.

If we're going to thrive in this space, we can't just chase trends, we have to anticipate them. That's what will keep our care relevant, ethical, and rooted in real value.

Chapter 4: Artificial Intelligence in Aesthetics: Opportunity or Threat?

Artificial intelligence isn't just coming. It's already here. And as nurse practitioners in aesthetic medicine and entrepreneurship, we have a choice: fear it, ignore it, or learn how to use it wisely.

AI is transforming the way we assess skin, plan treatments, and even interact with patients. Tools like 3D facial mapping, algorithm-powered skin analysis, and virtual simulation apps are becoming part of the modern aesthetic experience. These technologies help us visualize outcomes, track progress, and communicate more clearly with patients. When used correctly, AI can make our care safer, more personalized, and more efficient.

But we also need to be honest about the limitations and the risks. AI is only as good as the data it's trained on. If those datasets are biased or lack representation, the recommendations will be too. That means we must remain critical of tools that claim to "diagnose" or "predict" without transparent evidence behind them. As nurse practitioners, we bring the human lens. We ask the deeper questions. We recognize nuance, context, and identity in ways no algorithm can.

There's also the question of privacy and ethics. Patients trust us with intimate details about their appearance, health, and goals. Any AI tool we use must meet the same standards of confidentiality and informed consent that we uphold in every aspect of our practice.

We can't afford to be passive observers here. AI is moving fast, and aesthetic medicine is one of the industries most ripe for disruption. That's why we need to be in the room—testing these tools, asking the hard questions, and advocating for equitable, ethical tech development. It's not about replacing our expertise; it's about amplifying it.

PART II: SCOPE, TRAINING, AND CLINICAL READINESS

- **Who Can Practice Aesthetics? Know Your Scope**
    - A review of licensing, supervision, and key legal considerations to keep your practice safe and compliant.

- **Clinical Training - Evaluating Legitimacy**
    - A guide to identifying credible programs, red flags to avoid, and organizations that support high standards in NP-led aesthetic education.
    - Aesthetic NP Training Program Scorecard

- **Questions to Ask During Hands-On Training**
    - Make your training count. These are the questions you should be asking during hands-on sessions to ensure you're learning safely and effectively.
    - Aesthetic NP Competency Checklist

- **Understanding Race and Ethnicity in Aesthetic Care**
    - Delve into how race, ethnicity, and culture shape patient expectations and aesthetic outcomes, and why this knowledge is critical to ethical care.

PART II: SCOPE, TRAINING, AND CLINICAL READINESS

- **Cultural Considerations in Beauty and Aging**
    - This chapter explores how cultural identity, generational beliefs, and historical trauma influence the perception of aging and aesthetic intervention.

- **Anatomy and Physiology for Aesthetic Nurse Practitioners**
    - A clinical refresher tailored to facial and scalp anatomy, vascular mapping, and how to prevent complications in aesthetic procedures.

- **Patient Evaluation: Laying the Clinical Foundation**
    - From patient intake forms to skin assessments and contraindications, this chapter gives you the tools to conduct thorough, informed evaluations.

Chapter 5: Who Can Practice Aesthetics? Know Your Scope

Before we pick up a syringe or power on a laser, we need to get crystal clear on one thing: our scope of practice. Aesthetic medicine isn't a free-for-all. The rules that govern what we can do and how we can do it depend on where we live, our licensure, and the structure of our business. And as nurse practitioners, we hold both the privilege and the responsibility of practicing at the top of our license. That means being fully informed about the legal landscape and clinical expectations tied to aesthetic care.

In some states, NPs can operate independently, open their aesthetic practices, and perform procedures without physician oversight. In other cases, supervision or collaboration agreements are still required. Then there's the added complexity of delegating tasks to RNs, medical assistants, or estheticians within your practice. These decisions can impact your liability, your insurance, and ultimately, your patient safety.

Here's the key: know your state laws. Not what someone told you on Instagram. Not what worked for a colleague in another city. Not what a training company "assumed" was okay. You need to know what's allowed where you practice, and have documentation to back it up.

That includes:

- Who can own a medical spa
- Whether you need a Medical Director and their credentials
- What procedures fall under your scope (neuromodulators, fillers, laser, PRP, microneedling, etc.)
- What level of supervision or oversight is required
- How you can advertise and bill ethically

It's not glamorous, but it's non-negotiable. The fastest way to lose your license or your reputation is to skip the legal groundwork. If you're unsure, consult a healthcare attorney who specializes in aesthetic medicine. Remember: being an NP in aesthetics means we're blending clinical judgment with entrepreneurial leadership. Let's do so, legally, ethically, and with confidence.

Examples of What You Need to Know

Clinical and Medical Knowledge Competency

Foundational Knowledge

- Mastery of facial anatomy: bone structure, vasculature, muscle groups, fat pads, ligaments.
- Skin physiology and pathology, including the aging process and skin disorders relevant to aesthetics (e.g., melasma, PIH, acne scarring).
- Understanding differences in skin of color, including common misdiagnoses, treatment contraindications, and post-inflammatory responses.

Pharmacology and Device Literacy

- Mechanism of action, dosing, and side effects.
- Composition, properties, and indications for dermal fillers (e.g., HA vs. biostimulatory).
- Safety protocols and indications for energy-based devices (e.g., lasers, IPL, radiofrequency).

- Proper reconstitution, storage, and handling of injectable and topical agents.
- Recognition and management of complications such as vascular occlusion, granulomas, infections, and delayed hypersensitivity reactions.

Procedural and Technical Skills

Injection Techniques

- Competence in neurotoxin injections: glabellar complex, frontalis, orbicularis oculi, platysma, DAO, masseter.
- Filler techniques: linear threading, fanning, bolus, retrograde, cannula vs. needle decision-making.
- Volume restoration and contouring: lips, cheeks, jawline, chin, tear trough, and temples.

Adjunctive Procedures

- Chemical peels: superficial to medium depth, indication selection by skin type.
- Microneedling and microneedling radio frequency (RF).
- Platelet-rich plasma (PRP) and platelet-rich fibrin (PRF) therapy.
- Medical-grade facials, LED light therapy, and post-procedure protocols.

Complication Management

- Emergency protocol drills: vascular occlusion (Hyaluronidase use), anaphylaxis, infection management.
- Post-procedure instructions for swelling, bruising, delayed reactions, and patient education.

Scope of Practice

Defined by the intersection of:

- State Nurse Practice Act
- State Board of Nursing regulations
- Supervisory or collaborative agreements (where required)
- Practice setting policies and payer regulations

Clinical Scope

- Assessment and diagnosis of aesthetic concerns.
- Independent performance of non-invasive and minimally invasive cosmetic procedures (based on training and state law).
- Prescribing medications and topicals related to cosmetic care.

Prescriptive Authority

- Active NP license with controlled substance authority (if applicable).
- DEA registration where necessary.
- Compliance with state-specific requirements for prescriptive privileges in aesthetic settings.

Delegation and Supervision

- Delegation of tasks (e.g., device use, peels) must align with staff licensure and state law.
- NPs are responsible for protocol development and documentation of delegation.
- Some states require direct or indirect physician supervision for certain procedures or devices.

Action Step: Review your state Nurse Practice Act and Board of Nursing guidelines. Develop or revise your Standard Operating Procedures and delegation protocols accordingly.

Business and Practice Management Competencies

Practice Setup

- Legal business formation: PLLC, LLC, S-Corp considerations for NPs.
- Medical malpractice coverage specific to aesthetics.
- Vendor management and supplier contracts.
- Compliance with OSHA, HIPAA, and local health regulations.

Operational Efficiency

- Service pricing based on time, cost, and clinical complexity.
- Inventory and supply chain management.
- Financial literacy: Profit and Loss (P&L) review, budget forecasting, and revenue stream diversification.

Team Management

- Onboarding, training, and competency evaluation of clinical and administrative staff.
- Staff performance management and continuing education planning.
- Developing clinic workflows that support safety and profitability.

Ethical, Legal, and Cultural Competence

Ethical Practice

- Informed consent with specific procedural and product details.
- Transparent marketing and results representation.
- Appropriate referral of patients with unrealistic expectations or signs of body dysmorphic disorder (BDD).

Cultural Awareness

- Awareness in treating diverse skin types, especially darker skin tones.
- Awareness of varying aesthetic ideals and cultural beauty standards.
- Ensuring treatment recommendations and patient education is representative of the population

Risk Management

- Incident documentation, corrective action plans, and referral procedures.

- Regular review of malpractice cases in aesthetics to inform safety protocols.

Education, Research, and Lifelong Learning

Continuing Education

- Attend at least one clinical and one business-focused CME annually.
- Hands-on training from board-certified dermatologists, plastic surgeons, NPs or PAs with advanced experience.
- Shadowing or mentorship programs for advanced techniques or new modalities.

Research Literacy

- Ability to assess clinical trials, published safety data, and emerging technologies.
- Participation in or contribution to clinical or business research in aesthetic medicine.

Reflection: Which of your current skills are evidence-based, and which need to be updated based on new data or guidelines?

Where to Find Scope of Practice Information

1. **State Board of Nursing:** Each state's Board of Nursing outlines the scope of practice for NPs, including any collaborative agreement requirements and prescriptive authority. For example, the Texas Board of Nursing provides detailed information on APRN scope of practice and licensure requirements.
2. **State Medical Board:** Some aesthetic procedures fall under the jurisdiction of state medical boards. These boards may have specific regulations regarding who can perform certain cosmetic treatments, such as Botox or laser therapies. It's crucial to consult both the nursing and medical boards in your state to ensure compliance.
3. **American Association of Nurse Practitioners (AANP):** The AANP offers an interactive map detailing NP practice authority by state, categorizing them into full, reduced, or restricted practice environments. This resource provides a general overview but may not include specific details about aesthetic practices.
4. **Professional Organizations and Legal Resources:** Organizations like the American MedSpa Association (AmSpa) and legal firms specializing in healthcare law often provide updates and analyses on state-specific regulations affecting aesthetic NPs.

Understanding State Practice Environments

States are typically categorized into three types of NP practice authority. Learn more by visiting the National Council of State Boards of Nursing:

- **Full Practice:** NPs can evaluate patients, diagnose, interpret diagnostic tests, and initiate treatment plans independently.
- **Reduced Practice:** NPs must have a collaborative agreement with another health provider to provide patient care.
- **Restricted Practice:** NPs require supervision, delegation, or team management by another health provider.

Understanding your state's classification is essential to determining your level of autonomy.

Key Considerations for Aesthetic Nurse Practitioners

- **Collaborative Agreements:** In reduced or restricted states, NPs may need a formal agreement with a physician to perform or supervise certain procedures.
- **Procedure-Specific Regulations:** Some states have detailed rules regarding who can perform aesthetic treatments. Procedures like neuromodulator injections, dermal fillers, and energy-based device treatments may require specific training, certification, or physician oversight.

- **Ownership and Operation of Medical Spas**: State laws may also influence whether NPs can independently own or operate a medical spa. Some states require physician ownership or direct supervision for aesthetic practices.

Additional Resources

1. National Council of State Boards of Nursing (NCSBN)

The NCSBN provides national-level guidance on nursing regulations, including APRN practice. While it doesn't focus specifically on aesthetics, it's a useful reference for licensure, regulatory models, and scope standards.

2. American Nurses Association (ANA)

The ANA offers advocacy and educational resources that support nurse practitioners, especially in understanding scope of practice and professional boundaries. Their position statements often inform legislative discussions affecting NP autonomy.

3. International Society of Plastic and Aesthetic Nurses (ISPAN)

This organization supports nurses practicing in plastic and aesthetic surgery environments. It offers professional development, certifications, and best practices for safe, effective aesthetic care.

4. American Academy of Procedural Medicine (AAOPM)

Offers aesthetic training and certifications, often taken by NPs entering or expanding in aesthetics.

5. Cosmetic Injector's Association (CIA)

The Cosmetic Injector's Association is a professional organization dedicated to supporting the safety, education, and empowerment of licensed aesthetic injectors, including nurse practitioners. Their mission is to promote ethical, evidence-based practice while fostering community and collaboration among providers. CIA offers continuing education, advocacy tools, and a public-facing directory that helps elevate the visibility and credibility of certified injectors. It stands out for its emphasis on professional development and safety in the ever-evolving aesthetic landscape.

6. Facebook

You'll find several public and private communities where aesthetic NPs connect, collaborate, and support each other, both locally and nationally. These groups are great for asking questions, sharing resources, staying current with regulations, and getting real-world advice from peers. If you don't see one in your region, start your own to build community and establish yourself as a leader committed to elevating the profession. *Anyone can pretend to be someone they are not, when possible, ask for verification of credentials or only join pages that require it. Always do your own research.*

Chapter 6: Clinical Training - Evaluating Legitimacy

Once we understand what's within our scope, the next question becomes: *Where do we learn to do this work well?*

Here's what legitimate training looks like:

- Taught by experienced providers with credentials you can verify
- Includes anatomy, physiology, and complication management—not just marketing
- Provides hands-on practice under supervision
- Offers post-training support or mentorship
- Issues documentation that clearly states what was covered
- Aligns with current clinical guidelines and best practices

It should never be just about learning how to inject. It's about understanding when, *why*, and when not to. We also have to recognize that our learning doesn't end after one course. Aesthetic medicine is a specialty, and specialties require ongoing education. So yes, you'll need to invest in more than one training. That's part of the commitment we make when we decide to serve in this space. Seek out financial advisors and credible resources to increase your financial literacy, understanding of assessment accumulation, management, and estate planning.

When evaluating a program, ask:

- What's the trainer's background?
- Will I get to practice on live models?
- Is this course CME accredited?
- How are complications handled during training?
- Do they teach techniques for diverse skin tones and facial structures?

Before we drop thousands of dollars on training, let's talk strategy. Every course looks good online. Slick websites, beautiful before-and-after photos, promises of "six-figure success" in six months. But behind the gloss, we need to get clear on what we need to walk away with, skills, safety, and strategy.

Here's a list of questions you can ask before enrolling in any aesthetics training program:

Clinical Content

- Does the course cover facial anatomy and vasculature in depth?
- Are complications and emergency protocols included?
- Will I learn about skin of color and inclusive care?
- Does it include product education—not just Botox or filler, but neurotoxin types, rheology, and placement depth?

Hands-On Experience

- Are live model injections part of the training?
- Will I be supervised while injecting?
- How many models will I get to work on?
- Will I observe a variety of treatments—lips, cheeks, neuromodulators, etc.?

Post-Training Support

- Is mentorship offered after the course ends?
- Can I reach out with clinical questions?
- Do they provide ongoing CE opportunities or advanced courses?

Logistics & Legal

- Is the training tailored to my scope and state laws?
- Do I receive a certificate of completion that outlines what was taught?
- Is the course CME accredited?
- Are malpractice and model consent forms in place?

Representation, Identity & Impact

- Does the trainer have experience treating diverse populations?
- Are ethical considerations (body image, consent, safety) part of the curriculum?

Red Flags

If the answers are vague or overly salesy, that's your red flag. Also, watch out for "certification" scams. In the U.S., there's no official board certification in aesthetic injectables for NPs. So when someone says, "This is the only certified program in X," ask for details. It might be a proprietary credential, not a nationally recognized one. The right training protects your patients, your license, and your brand. Invest wisely.

We don't just need a certificate, we need competence. Training isn't about how quickly we can inject lips or how many Instagram followers the trainer has. It's about learning in a way that protects our patients, our licenses, and our future. Before clicking "purchase," pull out this **Aesthetic NP Training Program Scorecard** and make sure the program meets the mark. Because in aesthetics, there are no shortcuts—only safe steps forward.

Aesthetic NP Training Program Scorecard

Instructions: Read each question, then mark **Yes** or **No** on the next line. The more **Yes** responses, the stronger and more trustworthy the program.

1. Is the trainer an experienced provider with verifiable credentials?
   ☐ Yes ☐ No
2. Does the course include anatomy and physiology relevant to aesthetic procedures?
   ☐ Yes ☐ No
3. Are complications and risk management clearly taught?
   ☐ Yes ☐ No
4. Will I get hands-on practice under direct supervision?
   ☐ Yes ☐ No
5. Is post-training mentorship or follow-up support offered?
   ☐ Yes ☐ No
6. Will I receive documentation that outlines exactly what was covered?
   ☐ Yes ☐ No
7. Does the training align with current clinical guidelines and scope of practice'
   ☐ Yes ☐ No
8. Is the training CME-accredited or offered by a reputable organization?
   ☐ Yes ☐ No
9. Will I practice on live models in a controlled, supervised environment?
   ☐ Yes ☐ No
10. Are diverse skin tones and facial structures represented in the training?
    ☐ Yes ☐ No

How to Evaluate:

8–10 Yes: Strong program – highly recommended

5–7 Yes: Moderate – ask additional questions before enrolling

0–4 Yes: Likely inadequate – proceed with caution

Chapter 7: Questions to Ask During Hands-On Training

Hands-on training is where the magic happens, but only if we know how to make the most of it. Too often, we show up ready to observe and inject, but we leave with more questions than answers. This chapter is our reminder: we are not just students in the room, we are future aesthetic leaders. And leaders ask the right questions.

Here's a set of intentional, non-negotiable questions to bring into every hands-on training session:

1. **Anatomy in Action**
   - Can you walk me through the vascular danger zones in this injection site?
   - What are the depth and angle of injection here, and why?

2. **Product Knowledge**
   - What rheology does this filler have, and why are we choosing it for this area?
   - How long is this product expected to last, and how does it integrate into the tissue?

3. **Safety Protocols**
   - What are your immediate steps if vascular occlusion is suspected?
   - How do you counsel patients on risks without creating fear?

4. **Patient Selection**
   - What red flags would make you decline treatment today?
   - How do you assess for body dysmorphia or unrealistic expectations?

5. **Injection Technique**
   - What are you using as anatomical landmarks for this injection?
   - What do you look for to confirm proper placement?

6. **Consent & Documentation**
   - What should be included in a thorough informed consent?
   - How do you document adverse reactions or unusual outcomes?

7. **Cultural Sensitivity**
   - How do you modify your approach for patients with richly pigmented skin?
   - What considerations do you make when patients have cultural or religious norms around beauty?

Maintain a Spirit of Inquiry
The right training is only as valuable as the questions we ask. We don't need to impress anyone, we're here to protect our practice, elevate our skill set, and provide safe, inclusive care.

So bring your notebook (digital or hard copy), be curious, and don't be afraid to slow things down. Asking questions is how we build confidence, and that confidence becomes our reputation.

In the Appendix, You'll Find;
- Aesthetic NP Onboarding & Training Plan (60-90 Days)
- 4-Week Botox Training Roadmap for a New Aesthetic NP
- 4-Week Filler Training Roadmap for a New Aesthetic NP
- Botox & Filler Pricing Calculator (Based on Cost per Unit and Time)
- Sample Adverse Event SOP for an NP-Led Medical Spa

Aesthetic NP Competency Checklist

Organized into Core Domains. Mark off per quarter or training rotation.

I. Clinical Knowledge Competencies

Understands facial vascular and nerve anatomy

[ ] Proficient [ ] Needs Development

Notes: ______________________

Identifies high-risk injection zones

[ ] Proficient [ ] Needs Development

Notes: ______________________

Knows the pharmacology of toxins and fillers

[ ] Proficient [ ] Needs Development

Notes: ______________________

Describes common facial aging patterns by decade

[ ] Proficient [ ] Needs Development

Notes: ______________________

Applies Fitzpatrick skin typing accurately

[ ] Proficient [ ] Needs Development

Notes: ______________________

Can articulate aging differences in skin of color

[ ] Proficient [ ] Needs Development

Notes: ______________________

Knows safety protocols for energy-based devices

[ ] Proficient [ ] Needs Development

Notes: ______________________

II. Procedural Competencies

Full-face consultation and aesthetic assessment

[ ] Observed [ ] Supervised [ ] Independent

Notes: ______________________

Botox injection: glabella

[ ] Observed [ ] Supervised [ ] Independent

Notes: ______________________

Aesthetic NP Competency Checklist

Organized into Core Domains. Mark off per quarter or training rotation.

Botox injection: forehead

[ ] Observed [ ] Supervised [ ] Independent

Notes: ___________________________

Botox injection: crow's feet

[ ] Observed [ ] Supervised [ ] Independent

Notes: ___________________________

Lip filler (needle)

[ ] Observed [ ] Supervised [ ] Independent

Notes: ___________________________

Cheek filler (cannula)

[ ] Observed [ ] Supervised [ ] Independent

Notes: ___________________________

Chin/jawline contouring

[ ] Observed [ ] Supervised [ ] Independent

Notes: ___________________________

Biostimulant reconstitution and injection

[ ] Observed [ ] Supervised [ ] Independent

Notes: ___________________________

Hylenex reconstitution & emergency use

[ ] Observed [ ] Supervised [ ] Independent

Notes: ___________________________

Management of bruising, swelling, and patient education

[ ] Observed [ ] Supervised [ ] Independent

Notes: ___________________________

Post-care instructions tailored by procedure & patient

[ ] Observed [ ] Supervised [ ] Independent

Notes: ___________________________

III. Safety & Compliance Competencies

Aesthetic NP Competency Checklist

Organized into Core Domains. Mark off per quarter or training rotation.

Conducts and documents informed consent thoroughly

[ ] Proficient [ ] Needs Development

Notes: ____________________________

Maintains emergency kit and expiration checks

[ ] Proficient [ ] Needs Development

Notes: ____________________________

Familiar with occlusion protocols and rescue steps

[ ] Proficient [ ] Needs Development

Notes: ____________________________

Screens for Body Dysmorphic Disorder or unrealistic expectations

[ ] Proficient [ ] Needs Development

Notes: ____________________________

Documents injection procedure in chart (site, lot #, technique)

[ ] Proficient [ ] Needs Development

Notes: ____________________________

Follows OSHA standards for sharps and biohazard disposal

[ ] Proficient [ ] Needs Development

Notes: ____________________________

IV. Business & Legal Competencies

Reviewed Nurse Practice Act & aesthetic scope in state

[ ] Completed [ ] In Progress

Notes: ____________________________

Has collaborative or supervisory agreement if required

[ ] Completed [ ] In Progress

Notes: ____________________________

Created or reviewed aesthetic-specific SOPs

[ ] Completed [ ] In Progress

Notes: ____________________________

Uses HIPAA-compliant EMR and photo storage

[ ] Completed [ ] In Progress

Aesthetic NP Competency Checklist

Organized into Core Domains. Mark off per quarter or training rotation.

Notes: ______________________

Has malpractice coverage that includes aesthetics

[ ] Completed [ ] In Progress

Notes: ______________________

Created pricing based on time, product cost, and market

[ ] Completed [ ] In Progress

Notes: ______________________

V. Communication & Cultural Competencies

Explains aesthetic goals clearly and manages expectations

[ ] Proficient [ ] Needs Development

Notes: ______________________

Adapts procedures and products for skin of color

[ ] Proficient [ ] Needs Development

Notes: ______________________

Uses respectful language for cosmetic concerns (non-judgmental)

[ ] Proficient [ ] Needs Development

Notes: ______________________

Screens and adapts based on cultural or personal beauty norms

[ ] Proficient [ ] Needs Development

Notes: ______________________

Chapter 8: Understanding Race and Ethnicity in Aesthetic Care

If we're serious about delivering ethical, effective, and inclusive aesthetic care, then we must do more than memorize skin phototypes. We have to understand people, their lived experiences, cultural identities, and the ways race and ethnicity shape both aesthetic ideals and clinical outcomes.

This chapter isn't just about treating melanated skin, it's about shifting how we think, evaluate, and engage with every patient.

Race, Ethnicity, and Clinical Relevance
Let's start here: Race is not biology, but it often has biological consequences. Social determinants of health, access to care, environmental exposure, and generational trauma all influence how patients present and what they expect.

We've seen this play out in:

- Misdiagnosis of conditions like melasma or PIH because clinicians weren't trained on how they appear in skin of color.
- Poor outcomes from laser treatments because devices weren't tested on diverse skin tones.
- Undercorrection or overcorrection in aesthetic treatments due to assumptions about what features patients "should" want altered.

We're not here to "fix" features, we're here to enhance beauty with respect for identity.

Understanding Fitzpatrick Skin Type: A Critical Guide for Dermatology Nurse Practitioners

The Link Between Social Determinants of Health and Aesthetic Dermatology

Before we can transform lives through aesthetic care, we need to understand the real-life barriers and systemic factors that shape our patients' access to care, expectations, and outcomes. These aren't just clinical factors, they're societal. They're structural. They're deeply personal.

That's where the Social Determinants of Health (SDOH) come in.

What Are Social Determinants of Health?

Social determinants of health are the conditions in which people are born, live, learn, work, play, worship, and age. These factors directly impact health outcomes, often more than clinical interventions do.

They fall into five main domains:

1. Economic Stability – income, employment, debt, and access to financial resources
2. Education Access and Quality – literacy, health literacy, language proficiency, and educational opportunities
3. Health Care Access and Quality – availability of providers, insurance coverage, culturally competent care
4. Neighborhood and Built Environment – housing conditions, transportation, safety, and access to health-promoting spaces
5. Social and Community Context – support systems, social cohesion, experiences with discrimination, and civic participation

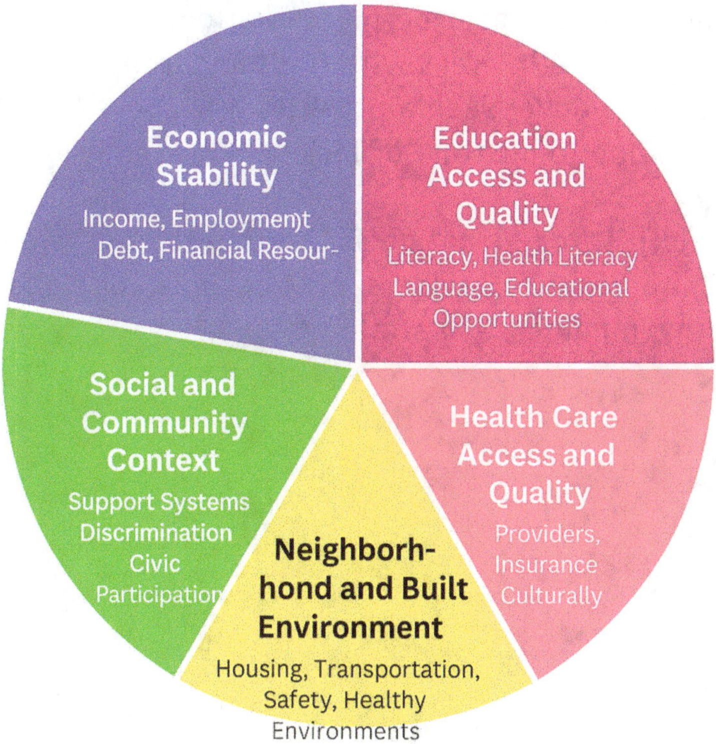

Each of these domains plays a role in shaping how, when, and whether patients seek care—including aesthetic dermatology.

Why SDOH Matters in Our Work
Let's be clear: Aesthetic care is health care. Skin health, self-image, and the ability to access elective procedures that enhance confidence are all part of overall well-being. But here's what often gets overlooked:

- A patient with limited income may prioritize rent over rosacea treatment, even though the skin condition impacts their mental health.
- A person facing chronic racial discrimination may experience higher stress levels, which can trigger or worsen conditions like acne, alopecia, or hyperpigmentation.
- Patients who live in areas with limited dermatology services or where they've never seen a provider who looks like them may delay care due to mistrust or lack of representation.

These are not just individual decisions. These are systemic realities that aesthetic providers must acknowledge and navigate with empathy, humility, and strategy.

Aesthetics and the Upstream Factors

We often think of aesthetics as the "downstream" end of care, elective, advanced, and out of reach for many. But when we take SDOH into account, we realize:

- Access to aesthetic services is a privilege shaped by upstream factors like wealth, transportation, insurance coverage, and racial bias.
- The decision to seek treatment may stem from deeper societal pressures or experiences with beauty standards shaped by colonialism, media, and Eurocentric norms.
- The outcomes we deliver, especially for skin of color, depend on our ability to understand context, not just skin type.

If we want to be inclusive providers, we can't ignore these realities. We have to lean into them, designing care plans, pricing models, and communication styles that honor the culture and heritage our patients bring with them.

How We Lead With Awareness

Here's how we bring an SDOH lens to aesthetic care:

- We ask open-ended questions that go beyond symptoms and appearance.
- We listen for clues about barriers, from financial insecurity to prior trauma in health care settings.
- We don't judge or assume, we partner.
- We advocate for access, for representation, and for education that closes the knowledge gap in underserved communities.

The goal isn't just flawless skin or a perfect contour. It's health care access for all. It's helping our patients feel confident, seen, and empowered on their terms.

Chapter 9: Cultural Considerations in Beauty and Aging

As aesthetic providers, we don't just work with skin, we work with stories. Every wrinkle, scar, and freckle tells part of someone's journey. And the way people interpret those stories is shaped by culture.

Beauty Isn't Universal: It's Cultural

Beauty standards aren't one-size-fits-all. What's considered youthful, attractive, or ideal in one culture might be completely different in another. If we want to offer aesthetic services with integrity, we need to recognize the deep cultural context behind each patient's goals and preferences.

The dominant aesthetic standards in Western medicine have historically centered on whiteness, thinness, youth, and European features. But our patients come from everywhere with diverse values, features, and priorities. Some cultures celebrate signs of aging. Others prize fuller figures or melanin-rich skin. Some communities see aesthetic treatments as taboo, while others embrace them as expressions of self-love and empowerment.

We don't get to decide what beauty means. Our role is to understand what it means to our patients and clients and help them feel more aligned with their own definition.

How Cultural Beliefs Shape Aesthetic Choices

Here are a few ways culture may influence aesthetic care:

- Aging gracefully vs. anti-aging treatments: In some cultures, aging is a sign of wisdom and status. In others, youth is idealized. We have to ask, not assume, what aging means to the patient sitting across from us.
- Facial features and ethnic identity: Aesthetic interventions like nose reshaping, lip fillers, or skin lightening can be complex when they intersect with racial identity and societal pressure. Our job is to hold space for those conversations without judgment.
- Attitudes toward "cosmetic" procedures: For some, aesthetic treatments are part of self-care. For others, they may carry religious, moral, or cultural implications. Understanding these views helps us build trust and offer appropriate recommendations.

Cultural Sensitivity Is a Non-Negotiable Skill

Being culturally aware doesn't mean knowing everything. It means staying curious, open-minded, and humble.

We can demonstrate this by:

- Asking patients how they define beauty, aging, and self-confidence.
- Being aware of how Eurocentric standards have influenced medical aesthetics, and doing the work to offer more inclusive options.
- Learning about the beauty rituals, skin concerns, and aesthetic traditions in different cultures.
- Challenging our own assumptions and biases, especially the ones we didn't realize we had.

Creating a Culturally Safe Space
Cultural safety is about creating a space where patients feel respected, not pressured to conform. It means asking questions like:

- “What does beauty mean to you?”
- “How do you want to feel when you look in the mirror?”
- “Are there any cultural or personal beliefs I should know before we explore treatment options?”

When we lead with those questions, we’re not just providing aesthetic care, we’re building a relationship that’s rooted in dignity, understanding, and choice.

Chapter 10: Anatomy and Physiology for Aesthetic Nurse Practitioners

Let's face it, when it comes to injecting, sculpting, or enhancing any part of the human face or body, our knowledge of anatomy is the foundation. We're not just artists, we're clinicians who must understand the structures we're working with and the risks we're mitigating.

This chapter isn't meant to be an anatomy textbook, but rather a clinical refresher tailored to what matters most in aesthetic practice.

Why Anatomy Matters in Aesthetics

Aesthetics is not just about knowing where to inject. It's about knowing where not to inject. Mastering facial layers, vasculature, muscle function, and fat compartments gives us the tools to:

- Prevent complications like vascular occlusion
- Customize treatment plans for unique facial anatomy
- Understand how aging changes facial structures
- Elevate our outcomes with precision and safety

When we understand anatomy, we instill trust and create better results.

Key Anatomical Areas in Aesthetic Practice

Let's focus on the areas most frequently treated and what every aesthetic NP should know.

Upper Face

- Frontalis: Main target for forehead lines. Understand how its contraction elevates brows and causes horizontal lines.
- Corrugator and procerus complex: Treating frown lines requires familiarity with this muscle group to avoid heavy brows or asymmetry.
- Orbicularis oculi: Key for crow's feet and periocular treatments. Important to assess dynamic movement and depth.

Midface

- Zygomaticus major/minor, levator labii superioris: These muscles lift the upper lip and cheek area. Improper filler placement here can affect smile symmetry.
- Infraorbital foramen: A critical landmark to avoid when treating tear troughs or under-eye areas.
- Deep vs. superficial fat pads: Know which compartments deflate with aging and which contribute to heaviness.

Lower Face

- Masseter and mentalis: Used in jawline contouring and chin balancing. Over-treatment can lead to changes in speech or chewing.
- Facial artery and vein courses: Especially relevant when using fillers around the nasolabial folds and lips.
- Risorius, depressor anguli oris: These affect marionette lines and lower face expressions.

Neck and Décolleté

- Platysma: Treating neck bands with neuromodulators requires clear identification of this muscle.
- Skin laxity, fat distribution, and vascular structures: All play a role in procedures like Kybella, RF microneedling, and skin tightening.

Understanding Physiology

Knowing anatomy is one part, understanding how the body responds to treatments is just as important.

- Neuromodulators work by blocking acetylcholine at the neuromuscular junction.
- Hyaluronic acid fillers integrate with tissue and attract water; how much depends on cross-linking and product selection.
- Collagen-stimulating treatments (like Sculptra or RF devices) initiate controlled trauma to encourage regeneration.
- Healing timelines and inflammatory responses affect patient outcomes, satisfaction, and re-treatment windows.

Clinical Application Tips

- Use ultrasound or anatomy apps regularly to stay sharp.
- Attend cadaver labs whenever possible; they're worth every penny.
- Don't skip the assessment phase: facial symmetry, movement, aging patterns, and patient goals all require your anatomical eye.
- Keep a running list of anatomical variations you notice. Patterns will emerge that make you more precise with time.

Bottom Line

You don't have to memorize every muscle or vessel, but you do need to approach your work with anatomical respect. Every injection is a medical procedure, and every face is a map. When we commit to understanding what's beneath the skin, we raise the bar for safety, skill, and satisfaction.

Chapter 11: Patient Evaluation—Laying the Clinical Foundation

Before we ever pick up a syringe or prepare a laser, our most powerful tools as aesthetic nurse practitioners are our eyes, ears, and intuition. Patient evaluation is where everything begins. It's how we lay the clinical foundation for ethical, effective, and personalized aesthetic care. When done right, it sets the tone for trust, safety, and satisfaction. And when skipped or rushed, it can compromise outcomes, confidence, and even our careers.

Why Evaluation Comes First

We don't just treat skin, we treat people. Each patient brings their history, hopes, fears, and unique anatomical canvas. A comprehensive evaluation isn't just about identifying wrinkles, volume loss, or pigmentation. It's about understanding the person in front of us. What are their goals? What is their lifestyle? What concerns are they not yet comfortable saying out loud?

When we take the time to listen and assess thoroughly, we show respect for the whole person, not just their appearance. That's where transformation truly begins.

The Essential Components of an Aesthetic Evaluation

Medical and Aesthetic History

We review medical history not just for contraindications but for context. Autoimmune conditions, medications, recent dental work, or a history of cold sores? All these influence what treatments we can offer and how we sequence them. Aesthetic history gives insight into what they've done before, what they liked or didn't, and what results they're seeking now.

Lifestyle and Daily Habits
Sun exposure, skincare routines, exercise, smoking, and sleep; these habits affect skin integrity and healing. When we know what they do every day, we can give recommendations that actually fit into their lives. That's how we create sustainable results.

Facial and Skin Assessment
We examine structure, tone, symmetry, texture, volume, and elasticity. We don't just zoom in, we step back. We assess from multiple angles and in different lighting, if needed. Understanding their baseline anatomy is crucial before making any changes.

Psychosocial Considerations
Aesthetic goals are emotional. Our patients may be navigating aging, divorce, postpartum changes, or career transitions. We listen for signs of body dysmorphia, unrealistic expectations, or external pressure. We can't always solve what's happening internally, but we can refer, support, and protect our patients from harm.

Photography and Documentation
Clinical photography is part of evaluation and essential to informed consent, tracking outcomes, and marketing. It also protects us legally. We take consistent, standardized photos—front, side, and oblique views—with good lighting and a neutral expression. These images are gold in both clinical care and practice-building.

Building Trust Through Evaluation

When we take the time to evaluate thoroughly, we show patients that we value their well-being over a quick procedure. That trust builds long-term relationships and turns one-time visits into ongoing care.

This is also the moment we educate. We explain how skin works, why we're recommending certain treatments, and what they can expect. We shift the focus from "quick fixes" to long-term skin health. That's how we position ourselves not just as providers, but as partners.

The Art of Saying "No"

One of the most powerful things we can say during an evaluation is "not today." Sometimes a patient isn't ready medically, emotionally, or financially. Sometimes the treatment they want isn't the one they need. Evaluation gives us the information and confidence to redirect or delay with professionalism and empathy. We never want to become a "yes clinic." We want to become *the right clinic*.

PART III: HERITAGE, IDENTITY, AND INFLUENCE

- **Aesthetic Preferences in Melanated Skin**
  - Explore the subtle (and not-so-subtle) differences in aesthetic goals among patients of color, and how cultural norms shape the desired results.

- **Aging in Skin of Color**
  - Understand the aging process in darker skin tones, including unique presentations and common misconceptions that affect treatment planning.

- **Perceptions of Beauty: Black, Latin, East & South Asian, Middle Eastern, and White Beauty Ideals**
  - A global perspective on beauty norms, their socio-cultural roots, and how they influence patients' choices in aesthetic care.

- **Social Media & The Nurse Practitioner's Role in Shaping Beauty Norms**
  - Instagram, TikTok, and the rise of "aspirational aesthetics." In this chapter, we explore how NPs can be responsible leaders in the beauty conversation.

Chapter 12: Aesthetic Preferences in Melanated Skin

Our industry hasn't always centered melanated skin. Historically, the aesthetic medicine narrative has been overwhelmingly shaped by Eurocentric beauty standards, with little regard for how those standards translate across the spectrum of skin tones and cultural identities. But things are shifting, and we are the ones helping lead that change.

As Nurse Practitioners entering this space, we need to recognize that patients with richly pigmented skin often have different aesthetic goals, skin responses, and risk profiles than what's typically taught in standard training. This isn't about separating people, it's about serving them more thoughtfully and thoroughly.

Listening First, Then Treating

When we sit across from a patient with melanated skin, our job isn't to assume what they want, it's to ask. For some, the goal might be a radiant, even-toned complexion without compromising the natural undertones that define their cultural beauty. Others might want to reduce the appearance of acne scars, soften lines, or address hair loss without changing their features.

Aesthetic preferences are often deeply personal, shaped by lived experience, community standards, and societal pressures. Our role is to listen carefully, ask open-ended questions, and build trust before we ever touch a syringe or a laser.

Understanding Skin Response

Here's where knowledge becomes power: melanated skin has unique physiological responses. It's more prone to postinflammatory hyperpigmentation (PIH), more reactive to inflammation, and may respond differently to certain treatments like chemical peels, microneedling, or lasers.

We can't afford to "wing it" here. Using improper techniques or devices not suited for darker skin tones can cause long-term harm, both physically and emotionally. It's our responsibility to not only seek out education in this area, but to make it standard in our practices.

Designing Inclusive Treatment Plans
When we co-create treatment plans with patients of color, we are doing more than improving appearance, we're reinforcing dignity. Inclusive care means we tailor our approach to their specific needs, using products and protocols that respect melanin-rich skin and reflect evidence-based safety standards.

For example, when considering hyperpigmentation treatments, we might prioritize topical agents like azelaic acid or tranexamic acid before turning to in-office procedures. If we do offer peels or lasers, we must choose ones that minimize thermal damage and inflammation. We always discuss the risks and set realistic expectations, so patients feel empowered, not disappointed.

Culture Matters
Remember, some patients of color have experienced medical gaslighting or aesthetic practices that made them feel invisible. We're not just addressing pigment or texture. We're building a new model of care that validates their beauty, history, and identity.
It starts with education, but it doesn't stop there. It's how we show up, how we market, how we train our teams, and how we advocate for inclusive representation at every level of this industry.
We are the next generation of aesthetic leaders.

Let's make sure our practices reflect the full spectrum of beauty, starting with how we honor and serve melanated skin.

Understanding Melanin-Rich Skin: Beyond Fitzpatrick

We've all heard of the Fitzpatrick scale, but let's be clear, it's a starting point, not the full story. Patients with melanated skin may fall into types III to VI, but their skin behavior, sensitivities, and aging patterns vary widely. This includes differences in:

- Collagen density and elasticity
- Propensity for hyperpigmentation or keloids
- Oil production and barrier function
- Response to light-based or ablative treatments

That means our approach must be tailored, not just to Fitzpatrick type, but to each patient's lived experience with their skin.

What Our Patients Want—and What They Don't

We've all seen the "cookie-cutter" aesthetic: overfilled cheeks, razor-sharp jawlines, and brows pulled sky-high. But when we listen to our melanated patients, we hear something different. Many of them are not trying to erase ethnicity, they're trying to enhance what already exists.

Common aesthetic preferences include:

- Skin tone evenness over lightening
- Natural contouring over exaggerated volume
- Youthful brightness without losing facial character
- Hair preservation, especially along the temples and hairline
- Texture refinement without compromising melanin

We've also heard loud and clear what patients don't want: to be "lightened," to look plastic, or to be treated like an aesthetic afterthought. This is where our sensitivity and cultural awareness become clinical skills, not just soft skills.

Conversations That Matter

Aesthetic evaluation for melanated patients isn't just about what we see, it's about what we ask. Are they concerned about pigmentation? Have they had a bad experience with lasers or peels? Are they being pressured to conform to Eurocentric beauty standards?

These conversations may be layered, emotional, and deeply personal. When we create space for them, we become more than providers, we become advocates.

Educating Without Shaming

Sometimes our patients come in with misconceptions. They may be using harmful products, like unregulated bleaching creams or harsh exfoliants. Rather than shame, we offer education. We explain how melanin protects, how inflammation leaves a deeper mark, and how we can achieve their goals safely and sustainably. Education builds empowerment, and empowered patients make better choices.

Treatment Planning with Intention

When working with melanated skin, less is often more. Our treatment plans prioritize:

- Barrier support and hydration
- Gradual brightening with agents like azelaic acid, kojic acid, or tranexamic acid

- Non-ablative lasers or energy-based devices with melanin-safe settings
- Injectables that respect facial proportions and honor cultural identity

We approach every treatment with caution, clarity, and care. Because the stakes are higher, and the rewards, when done right, are beautiful.

The Key to Successful Treatments for Skin of Color
Building rapport is one of the most crucial steps in ensuring that your patients feel seen, heard, and valued, especially when working with individuals with skin of color. Establishing trust takes intentional effort and communication, but it's worth it. When patients feel that you understand their unique skin needs and concerns, they're more likely to share their true desires and expectations, which leads to better outcomes. As Aesthetic NPs, we should make rapport-building a top priority. It not only enhances the treatment experience but also fosters long-term relationships with our patients, ensuring they return to us for the care they can't get just anywhere. Trust isn't given; it's earned through thoughtful, culturally sensitive care.

Feel Like You Can't Relate?
For providers who are not of color, it's essential to approach the treatment of patients with skin of color with transparency, humility, and a commitment to continuous learning. Acknowledge the potential knowledge gap openly, this will help establish trust. If you're not confident or comfortable with a treatment or procedure, refer the patient to someone who specializes in treating skin of color. However, don't let uncertainty stop you from engaging with your patients. Be transparent about your limitations, but let your willingness to learn and grow show.

Listen to your patients with an open mind, and seek mentorship from those with more experience treating diverse skin tones. Investing in ongoing education and training on skin of color is crucial, not only because it's an ethical imperative, but also because there simply aren't enough providers who specialize in treating these patients. This presents a unique opportunity for all of us, regardless of background, to ensure that we can meet the needs of every patient. By building competency and confidence in treating skin of color, we not only create a more inclusive and effective healthcare environment but also position ourselves to build a positive reputation in the community and within the profession. When patients see that you are genuinely committed to learning and providing excellent care, word will spread, and you'll earn the trust of diverse populations, enhancing both your practice and your professional standing.

Understanding Fitzpatrick Skin Type: A Critical Guide for Dermatology Nurse Practitioners

One of the most referenced tools in our field is the Fitzpatrick Skin Phototype System, a framework that has guided clinical decisions for decades. But like many longstanding models, it deserves a closer look. Here, we'll explore its origins, examine its limitations, and unpack what it means when we talk about "skin of color."

What Is Skin Phototyping?

Skin phototyping was originally developed to categorize how skin responds to ultraviolet (UV) exposure, particularly in the context of phototherapy. Before the 1970s, classifications were often based on visual skin color alone, a method we now know is inadequate. In 1975, Dr. Thomas B. Fitzpatrick introduced a more dynamic model based on sunburn and tanning history. The Fitzpatrick system was revolutionary for its time, helping clinicians estimate safe starting doses for phototherapy.

The system classified skin into six types, from I (very fair, always burns) to VI (deeply pigmented, never burns). However, phototypes V and VI were added later and primarily based on visual skin color rather than physiological response. This mix of subjective and objective criteria introduced a range of interpretive challenges that persist today.

The Biology Behind the Model

Understanding skin phototype requires a grasp of two types of skin color: constitutive and facultative. Constitutive color is your genetic baseline, what you're born with. Facultative color is influenced by your environment, like sun exposure or hormonal changes. Both are important, but neither fully determines how skin will respond to UV light.

Melanin, specifically eumelanin and pheomelanin, plays a key role. Eumelanin, found in higher levels in darker skin, offers more effective UV protection. Pheomelanin, more common in lighter skin, is less protective and can even generate reactive oxygen species. Beyond melanin, other mechanisms like antioxidant enzymes and DNA repair systems contribute to photoprotection.

Honoring the Legacy, Recognizing the Limits

Dr. Fitzpatrick was a pioneer whose contributions shaped modern dermatology. From authoring the first multi-author dermatology textbook to identifying the melanosome and promoting photochemotherapy, his legacy is substantial. But the Fitzpatrick system, like all models, is not without flaws.

The original intent was to estimate the Minimal Erythema Dose (MED), the smallest amount of UV radiation needed to cause redness in the skin. MED varies widely based on melanin content, making it difficult to generalize across populations. While the Fitzpatrick system served as a helpful proxy, it doesn't always align with actual skin biology, especially in individuals with richly pigmented skin.

The Clinical Challenge

Many clinicians rely on the Fitzpatrick system for decision-making, yet the way we use it is often inconsistent. The questionnaire includes ten items across three categories: genetic traits, sun exposure reaction, and tanning habits. Yet in practice, we often reduce it to just one or two questions, or worse, assumptions based on appearance.

This creates gaps in care. For example, the system doesn't reliably predict post-inflammatory hyperpigmentation (PIH) or skin cancer risk in patients with skin of color. Nor does it guide treatment planning for cosmetic procedures with precision. As a result, nurse practitioners must look beyond Fitzpatrick and integrate a broader understanding of cutaneous biology and lived experience.

Selecting Safe Cosmetic Procedures in Skin of Color

I published an article on the **Mahogany Dermatology** blog on my recommendations for dermatology textbooks for skin of color, highlighting over ten essential medical texts that should be on the required reading list for nursing and medical schools. Despite the collection, there remains a significant gap, particularly in nursing, wound care, pediatric dermatology, and cosmetic dermatology.

One standout resource is Procedures in Cosmetic Dermatology: Cosmetic Procedures in Skin of Color by Dr. Andrew F. Alexis, a leader in dermatology. Alexis et al. (2024) offer evidence-based techniques for treating conditions like melasma, hyperpigmentation, and keloids, making this book an invaluable resource for dermatology nurse practitioners committed to safe and effective aesthetic care for all skin tones (Alexis et al., 2024).

To minimize post-procedure complications, the authors recommend collecting a thorough history that includes asking about hypertrophic scarring, keloids, and hyperpigmentation before performing cosmetic procedures. When it comes to skin typing, the authors recommend the **Roberts Skin Type Classification**, a four-part approach that evaluates phototype, hyperpigmentation, photoaging, and scarring through ancestral and clinical history and visual examination (Alexis et al., 2024).

The Roberts Skin Type Classification System

The Roberts Skin Type Classification System is a comprehensive tool designed to assess an individual's risk of adverse skin reactions following cosmetic procedures and inflammatory skin conditions. Unlike traditional skin typing methods, this system integrates four key indices: **skin phototype, photoaging severity, hyper/hypopigmentation risk, and scarring (hypertrophic scars and keloids) propensity** to predict potential complications and guide personalized treatment plans.

By evaluating these factors, clinicians can proactively identify patients at risk for PIH, scarring, or other sequelae, allowing for tailored interventions that minimize complications. This classification is particularly valuable for individuals with darker skin tones, who may be more prone to PIH and scarring. Additionally, it serves as a predictive model for treatment response, enabling practitioners to optimize outcomes by selecting the most suitable cosmetic procedures and pre/post-treatment care. By incorporating ancestral background, clinical history, and test site reactions, the Roberts system provides a multidimensional approach to skin assessment, enhancing both safety and efficacy in dermatologic and aesthetic treatments (Roberts, 2008, 2009).

Alternative Skin Typing Systems for Improved Risk Assessment

Several skin typing systems go beyond the Fitzpatrick scale by incorporating ancestry, pigmentation tendencies, and post-procedure risks to enhance treatment planning:

- **Lancer Ethnicity Scale**: Considers racial and ancestral background alongside Fitzpatrick phototypes to guide laser resurfacing treatments.
- **Fanous Skin Classification**: Accounts for ancestral origin and skin color to predict procedural risks and expected outcomes.
- **Goldman World Classification Scale**: Includes ancestry, Fitzpatrick type, and patient-reported tendencies for postinflammatory hyperpigmentation.
- **Taylor Hyperpigmentation Scale**: Uses a set of 15 color cards with varying pigmentation levels to visually assess and track hyperpigmentation severity, though results may vary between raters.
- **Roberts Skin Type Classification**: A four-part system incorporating Fitzpatrick phototype, Glogau photoaging scale, hyperpigmentation risk, and scarring tendency to predict post-procedure responses and optimize treatment planning (Gupta & Sharma, 2019; Roberts, 2009).

Moving Forward with Intention

As aesthetic and dermatology nurse practitioners, our goal isn't to abandon tools like the Fitzpatrick system, but to use them more critically and supplement them with holistic assessments. That means asking better questions, acknowledging the cultural context of beauty and skin health, and recognizing that one size never fits all. The future of dermatology lies in precision and personalization. And that future starts with us, by committing to inclusive education, staying informed about new research, and advocating for better models that serve all our patients with the dignity and expertise they deserve.

Chapter 13: Aging in Skin of Color

Let's challenge a common myth right now: melanated skin doesn't age. The truth is, all skin ages; it just ages differently. And if we're serious about offering culturally sensitive and clinically safe care, we need to understand exactly how and why that happens.

As Nurse Practitioners stepping into aesthetics, it's our job to help patients age on their terms, not based on outdated stereotypes or one-size-fits-all treatment plans. Skin of color deserves more than generic advice, it deserves nuanced, evidence-informed support.

The Beauty and Biology of Melanin

Melanin is powerful. It provides a natural photoprotective effect that can delay the onset of wrinkles, pigmentary changes, and visible signs of aging. People with darker skin tones often retain firmer, smoother skin for longer due to increased collagen density and slower collagen degradation. That's an advantage worth celebrating.

But it doesn't mean aging doesn't happen, it simply shows up differently. For example, while fine lines may appear later, volume loss, hollowing, uneven pigmentation, and laxity around the mouth or jawline can still occur and can be especially distressing for patients who've been told they're "too young" or "too pigmented" to age.

Hyperpigmentation Over Wrinkles

In lighter skin types, aging is often framed around wrinkles and laxity. In skin of color, it's hyperpigmentation and uneven tone that often take center stage.

Melanocytes are more reactive in darker skin, which means even a small trauma, like acne, an insect bite, or an improperly performed laser, can leave behind dark spots that last for months or years. Aging in these patients often looks like accumulated pigmentation and textural changes, not just sagging skin. When we shift our aesthetic approach to reflect this reality, our patients feel seen and our outcomes improve.

Building Culturally Intelligent Treatment Plans

We can't approach aging in skin of color with a copy-and-paste model. Treatment protocols that are safe and effective in lighter skin tones may need to be modified, or avoided altogether, in patients with melanin-rich skin.

Here's what we prioritize:

- Preventive strategies: Daily sunscreen use, antioxidant-rich skincare, and early collagen preservation.
- Antioxidants like vitamin C and E to fight environmental stressors
- Gentle resurfacing treatments: Microneedling, low-concentration chemical peels, and certain radiofrequency devices that are proven safe for darker skin tones.
- Pigment-conscious injectables: For dermal fillers and neuromodulators, we focus on subtle, natural results and educate our patients about the role these tools play in maintaining facial harmony, not changing identity.
- Patient education: Many patients of color are unfamiliar with how aesthetic aging presents in their skin. When we take time to explain the process with empathy and clarity, we build trust and inspire long-term engagement.

Aging Gracefully, Authentically, and Safely
In skin of color, the margin for error is smaller. Aggressive treatments can lead to permanent pigmentation issues or scarring.

That's why we practice:

- Conservative dosing
- Thoughtful product selection
- Deep patient education and follow-up

When we care for aging skin of color with intention, we become trusted partners, not just providers. We're not here to fix flaws; we're here to reveal radiance.

Representation and Reclamation
The beauty industry has spent decades ignoring how aging affects people of color, or worse, assuming we don't age at all. That lack of representation has left a lot of patients feeling disconnected from aesthetic care altogether.

But we're not here to uphold outdated beauty narratives. We're here to elevate new ones. When we talk openly about the unique aspects of aging in melanated skin, we're not just filling a knowledge gap, we're validating lived experience and empowering more people to age with intention. This is our moment to normalize aging as a full-spectrum journey. And that starts by seeing, respecting, and skillfully caring for skin in every shade.

Chapter 14: Perceptions of Beauty: Black, Latin, East & South Asian, Middle Eastern, and White Beauty Ideals

Beauty is never just skin deep, it's cultural, generational, and deeply personal. As aesthetic nurse practitioners, we can't offer meaningful, respectful care without understanding the diverse beauty ideals that shape our patients' desires. Our work doesn't just change appearances, it impacts identity, belonging, and self-worth.

We can't assume everyone wants a snatched jawline or plump lips. We must learn what beauty means to them, across cultures, skin tones, and lived experiences.

Why Beauty Ideals Matter in Aesthetic Practice

Each patient enters our space with a beauty blueprint shaped by:

- Family and cultural heritage
- Regional norms and global influences
- Media and social platforms
- Personal experiences with race, gender, and identity

Understanding these ideals allows us to:

- Avoid bias and assumptions
- Offer culturally congruent care
- Build trust by aligning treatments with the patient's vision of beauty

Let's explore what that can look like across different groups, knowing that within each category lies immense nuance and individuality.

Black Beauty Ideals

For many Black women and men, beauty is power, but it's also resistance. Historically excluded from mainstream beauty narratives, Black aesthetics have carved their own lane: bold, expressive, and rooted in legacy.

Common values and preferences may include:

- Smooth, even skin tone—hyperpigmentation is a frequent concern
- Defined cheekbones and jawlines
- Full lips and natural hair are embraced as beautiful
- Desire for glow and radiance over skin lightening or aggressive contouring

It's essential to be aware of colorism and texturism, systems that value lighter skin and looser curls, and not unintentionally reinforce them through treatment plans.

Latinx Beauty Ideals

In Latin cultures, beauty is often tied to sensuality and strong family or religious values. There's a mix of Indigenous, African, and European influences, creating a rich aesthetic tapestry.

Common features and goals may include:

- Smooth skin with warmth and vibrancy
- High cheekbones and expressive eyes
- Balanced, natural-looking lip enhancement
- Preservation of youth with subtle refinement

For some, beauty maintenance is a family tradition passed down through generations. These patients may arrive already educated and proactive about care.

East & South Asian Beauty Ideals

There's a growing wave of East and South Asian patients seeking aesthetic care, and their goals often differ from Western norms. Beauty here can be more subtle, symmetrical, and preservation-focused.

East Asian beauty standards may highlight:

- Clear, luminous skin is often described as "glass skin"
- Soft contours with less emphasis on angular features
- Minimalist, natural enhancements

South Asian patients may prioritize:

- Brightening uneven tone or melasma
- Sculpted brows, jawline, and cheeks
- Cultural or religious considerations, such as modesty or natural appearance

Both groups are often highly informed and cautious of pigment changes, making education and conservative treatment essential.

Middle Eastern Beauty Ideals

Middle Eastern patients often value striking features: dramatic eyes, high brows, and bold contours. Beauty here is celebrated with elegance, and often includes:

- Sharp jawlines and well-defined cheekbones
- Smooth skin texture and radiant tone
- Body contouring and balanced proportions

These patients may desire transformative results, but expect artistry and discretion. Listening deeply to their aesthetic goals is key.

White Beauty Ideals
While "Western" beauty ideals have influenced global aesthetics, they're not monolithic. Preferences shift across regions and generations.

Common patterns may include:

- Youthfulness through volume and skin tightening
- Preventative care with injectables
- Lash, lip, and brow enhancements for symmetry and expressiveness

However, growing movements toward natural aging, minimalism, and inclusive wellness are changing what beauty means.

Delivering Culturally Attuned Care
We don't have to be experts in every culture, but we must be curious, open, and respectful.

We ask questions like:

- "How do you define beauty?"
- "What do you love most about your appearance?"
- "Are there any features or results you'd like to preserve?"

This is how we build trust. This is how we deliver care that honors the whole person, not just the surface.

Chapter 15: Social Media & The Nurse Practitioner's Role in Shaping Beauty Norms

Whether we like it or not, social media is the new waiting room. It's where patients discover treatments, research providers, and decide what "beautiful" looks like. As aesthetic nurse practitioners, we're not just treating faces, we're shaping perceptions, influencing expectations, and setting standards.

That means we carry tremendous responsibility. Because what we post doesn't just promote our work, it promotes ideals.

We're More Than Just Providers—We're Influencers

Every before-and-after, every caption, every reel contributes to the collective idea of what's desirable, attainable, or worth pursuing.

Social media allows us to:

- Educate the public about safe, ethical aesthetic care
- Celebrate diverse forms of beauty and disrupt narrow beauty standards
- Correct misinformation and demystify the "behind the scenes" of injectables and skincare
- Showcase our expertise and artistry in a way that builds trust and attracts aligned patients

But it can also contribute to:

- Unrealistic expectations when filters distort results
- Body dysmorphia and comparison fatigue in vulnerable populations
- Overmedicalization of normal features when everything becomes something to "fix"

We have to walk the line between inspiration and integrity. We don't have to shrink our visibility, but we do need to stand in our values.

What We Post Matters

We've all seen the overly curated feeds: rows of perfect faces, identical lips, and filter-smooth skin. But real beauty is diverse. It's lived-in. It's shaped by culture, age, personality, and preference.

When we intentionally post:

- A wide range of skin tones and facial features
- Diverse ages and gender expressions
- Thoughtful captions about decision-making and patient values
- Transparent discussions around healing, downtime, or risks

...we create a safer and more inclusive space. We become the practitioners patients trust, not just the one with the pretty pictures.

Let's Talk About Trends

Social media thrives on novelty, and so do aesthetic trends. But not every trend should become a treatment plan. From the "fox eye" lift to exaggerated jawlines, we've all had to explain the limits (and risks) of chasing virality.

As professionals, we must:

- Evaluate trends through a clinical, ethical lens
- Help patients distinguish temporary fads from timeless beauty
- Protect our patients from over-treatment or regret
- Use trends as a conversation starter, not a sales tactic

We're allowed to be trendy, but we should never trade trust for likes.

Using Social Media for Advocacy
Let's not underestimate our power. Social media is also a tool for health awareness and advocacy.

We can:

- Raise awareness about skin of color concerns and disparities
- Normalize care for men, nonbinary folks, and underrepresented communities
- Share evidence-based information in a digestible, relatable way
- Collaborate with others to create aesthetic spaces that feel safe and seen

If we don't show up and speak up, the industry stays the same. But when we use our platforms with purpose, we make beauty better for everyone.

Our Bottom Line: Show Up with Integrity
We're not influencers first. We're nurses. That means we lead with care, ethics, and education, even online.

Let's be practitioners who:

- Reflect diverse beauty, not just trendy beauty
- Empower patients with realistic, informed choices
- Use our platform to build community, not competition

Because in this digital age, our content might be the first encounter someone has with aesthetic medicine. Let's make sure it's one worth trusting.

PART IV: CLINICAL CONDITIONS IN AESTHETIC PRACTICE

- ·**Skin Texture Concerns**
  - Discuss the clinical causes of uneven skin texture and how to evaluate patients seeking smoother skin.

- ·**Dermatosis Papulosa Nigra**
  - Clinical characteristics, treatment options, and post-treatment considerations in patients with richly pigmented skin.

- ·**Acne and Postinflammatory Hyperpigmentation (PIH)**
  - How to assess, manage, and minimize PIH risk in patients with acne-prone skin, especially in skin of color.

- ·**Melasma: Pathophysiology and Management**
  - A deep dive into one of the most misunderstood pigmentary disorders and evidence-based strategies for long-term management.

- ·**Alopecia and Scalp Concerns**
  - From traction alopecia to CCCA, this chapter explores the most common types of hair loss you'll encounter and how to approach them.

PART IV: CLINICAL CONDITIONS IN AESTHETIC PRACTICE

- **Hair Removal in Skin of Color**
    - Best practices, laser safety, and complications to avoid when providing hair removal services to diverse populations.

- **Hypertrophic Scars and Keloids**
    - Prevention, treatment modalities, and how to counsel patients predisposed to these scarring patterns.

- **Periorbital Rejuvenation**
    - Learn to evaluate and treat the delicate under-eye area, including common complaints and non-surgical options.

Chapter 16: Skin Texture Concerns
Understanding, Evaluating, and Treating Uneven Skin

We all want to help our patients put their best face forward, literally. But when it comes to texture, there's no one-size-fits-all solution. Whether our patients are concerned about roughness, scarring, or dullness, it's our job to get to the root of the issue, not just smooth over the surface.

What Do We Mean by "Texture"?

When patients say their skin feels "rough," "bumpy," or "not smooth," they're often pointing to a broad category of concerns, including:

- Enlarged pores
- Acne scarring (atrophic, hypertrophic, keloid)
- Milia or keratosis pilaris
- Dryness or dehydration
- Uneven tone that looks like uneven texture
- Fine lines that disrupt light reflection

Sometimes it's tactile, sometimes it's visual, and sometimes it's both. That's why a thorough assessment is key.

Clinical Causes of Uneven Skin Texture

Let's talk about what's going on under the surface:

- Excess keratin buildup: Leads to clogged pores and rough patches.
- Impaired barrier function: Causes flakiness, dullness, and reactive sensitivity.
- Chronic inflammation: Acne, eczema, or rosacea can disrupt collagen and create unevenness.

- Scarring from past trauma: This includes post-acne marks, especially in skin of color, where hyperpigmentation often accompanies scarring.
- Aging and sun exposure: Collagen loss, solar elastosis, and pigmentation changes make texture concerns more visible.

Patient Evaluation: Dig Deeper Than the Surface

When evaluating skin texture concerns, we want to assess both structure and behavior.

Ask yourself:

- Is this patient exfoliating too much or too little?
- Are they sensitized or compromised (barrier damage)?
- Do they have a history of acne or inflammatory skin conditions?
- Are there lifestyle factors like smoking, stress, or lack of sleep contributing to dullness?

Also, consider:

- Skin phototype
- Cultural skincare practices
- Medication history
- Previous cosmetic treatments

We're not just looking at what's visible, we're uncovering why the skin is behaving this way.

Treatment Options: Building the Right Texture Protocol

Every plan starts with education. Patients often expect immediate, dramatic results, but consistency and patience are our best tools. Treatment modalities we may consider include:

- Topical Retinoids: Gold standard for improving texture and cell turnover
- Chemical Peels: Tailored by depth and formulation; must be cautious with darker skin types
- Microneedling: Excellent for acne scars and collagen remodeling
- Laser Resurfacing: Use caution with melanated skin; fractional and non-ablative options are safer
- Hydrafacials and Enzyme Exfoliants: Gentler ways to renew the skin's surface without triggering irritation

Texture + Skin of Color: Proceed with Precision

For patients with richly pigmented skin, uneven texture often coexists with hyperpigmentation. That means we must:

- Treat slowly and conservatively
- Prioritize barrier support before aggressive resurfacing
- Monitor for PIH risk with every modality

Education goes a long way here. When we set realistic expectations and explain the "why" behind our method, we earn trust and better outcomes. Texture is more than skin-deep. It reflects lifestyle, inflammation, past trauma, and even confidence. When we take a personalized, strategic approach, we're not just smoothing the surface, we're restoring balance and helping patients feel more like themselves.

Chapter 17: Dermatosis Papulosa Nigra
Clinical Considerations for Treating Benign Lesions in Skin of Color

Let's talk about those small, smooth, dark papules that show up mostly on the cheeks, temples, and necks of our patients, especially those with richly pigmented skin. Dermatosis Papulosa Nigra (DPN) is a common and benign condition, but it's not always understood or treated with the care it deserves. As aesthetic NPs, we have a responsibility to approach DPNs with both clinical excellence and cultural sensitivity.

What Is Dermatosis Papulosa Nigra?

DPN is a variant of seborrheic keratosis, commonly seen in individuals with darker skin tones. These lesions are typically:

- Smooth or slightly rough
- Flat or pedunculated
- Brown to black in color
- 1–5 mm in size
- Gradually increasing in number over time

They are more prevalent in people of African, Asian, or Hispanic descent and often begin to appear in early adulthood, becoming more numerous with age.

Evaluation: When Patients Bring It Up

Most patients with DPN come to us not because the lesions are painful, but because they're visible and unwanted. Some may worry they're abnormal or even cancerous, while others simply want a more even appearance.

Here's what we evaluate:

- Number and distribution: Are they localized or widespread?
- Lesion type: Are they uniform in appearance or are there atypical features?
- Skin history: Is there a history of keloids, scarring, or hyperpigmentation?
- Patient goals: Is this purely cosmetic, or are they experiencing irritation?

Make no assumptions; some patients are proud of their DPN or view it as a family trait, while others want every last lesion removed. Our role is to assess, educate, and guide.

Treatment Options: Choose Wisely

Because DPN is benign, treatment is elective. But if removal is desired, we have several options, each requiring a careful, skin-of-color–specific approach to minimize scarring and pigment disruption.

Common modalities:

- Electrosurgery: Often used with a fine tip to remove or flatten lesions; requires a steady hand and post-care instructions to reduce PIH.
- Curettage: Effective for raised lesions; may be combined with electrosurgery.
- Laser therapy (Nd:YAG or CO_2): Can work well but carries a risk of pigment alteration if not done conservatively.
- Cryotherapy: Use with extreme caution; the risk of hypopigmentation is high in darker skin tones.

Always prep the skin, protect the surrounding tissue, and consider pre-treatment with melanin suppressants like hydroquinone if there's a history of PIH.

Post-Treatment Considerations

Our job doesn't end when the lesions are gone. Post-treatment care is critical, especially when treating melanated skin.

Key steps:

- Hydration and barrier repair: Non-comedogenic ointments, ceramides, and gentle cleansers.
- Sun protection: Daily Tinted SPF 50+ is non-negotiable. UV exposure increases PIH risk.
- Follow-up: Reassess healing, pigmentation changes, and patient satisfaction.

And don't forget the emotional component. DPN removal can be incredibly empowering, but it can also bring up feelings related to identity, aging, and cultural norms. Be present and listen.

A Note on Cultural Awareness

Some patients may have been told by other providers that DPN is "just cosmetic" or "not worth treating." Others may have had traumatic treatment experiences. As aesthetic NPs, we set a new standard when we approach skin of color with skill, respect, and informed consent. By offering evidence-based options and partnering with our patients on their terms, we show that aesthetic care is not just about beauty, it's about dignity.

Chapter 18: Acne and Post-inflammatory Hyperpigmentation: Managing Acne in Skin of Color Without Compromising Pigment Integrity

Acne is more than a rite of passage, it's one of the most common conditions we see in aesthetic practice. But when we're caring for patients with richly pigmented skin, there's another layer of complexity: post-inflammatory hyperpigmentation (PIH). We're not just clearing breakouts, we're also protecting pigment, self-esteem, and quality of life.

Understanding Acne in Skin of Color

While acne affects all ethnicities, patients with skin of color often experience:

- Inflammatory papules and pustules (more than comedonal acne)
- Higher risk of PIH from even mild lesions
- Longer healing times for pigment changes
- A heightened emotional burden due to visible marks and color contrast

Many of our patients come to us after years of over-the-counter products, misdiagnoses, and failed treatments that never accounted for their skin tone. This is due to the lack of representation in dermatology when it comes to:

- Education
- Faculty
- Medical images
- Clinical trials, inclusion criteria, and participant sampling
- Marketing
- Legislation and regulatory standards

What Is PIH and Why Does It Matter?

PIH is the skin's response to inflammation or injury. Melanocytes go into overdrive, creating dark spots after acne heals. This can last months (or years) and is often more distressing than the acne itself.

For aesthetic NPs, this means we need to:

- Treat acne early and effectively to prevent PIH and scarring
- Avoid aggressive treatments that can make pigment worse
- Tailor protocols specifically for melanin-rich skin
- Address the impact on mental and emotional health

Patient Evaluation: It Starts with Listening

We take a thorough, patient-centered approach:

- History: Onset, triggers, family history, previous treatments
- Lifestyle: Skincare habits, dietary influences, stress levels
- Skin phototype
- Scarring and PIH presence: Where is the pigment? Is it improving?
- Goals: Are they more bothered by active lesions or dark marks?

Always ask, never assume. Some patients are actively breaking out; others are just trying to fade the aftermath.

Treatment Strategy: Two Goals, One Plan

To manage acne and prevent PIH, we focus on calming inflammation, supporting the skin barrier, and gradually evening tone.

First-Line Acne Treatments for Skin of Color:

- Topical retinoids (adapalene, tretinoin): Start low and slow to avoid irritation
- Benzoyl peroxide (BPO): Use cautiously, always paired with moisturizers
- Topical antibiotics: Often in combo with BPO or retinoids
- Azelaic acid: Anti-inflammatory, pigment-regulating, and pregnancy safe
- Oral options: Spironolactone, doxycycline, or hormonal therapy when appropriate

Addressing PIH Simultaneously:

- Sunscreen: Daily Tinted SPF 50+ is foundational—no negotiation
- Hydroquinone (short-term use) or alternatives like kojic acid, niacinamide, and licorice root extract
- Chemical peels (superficial, like glycolic or lactic acid): Only when the skin is stable
- Laser? Caution. Use only if experienced and with the right wavelength (e.g., 1064 nm Nd:YAG)

Remember, our patients want results, but they don't want hypopigmentation, burns, or flare-ups in the process. We protect the melanin while correcting the problem.

The Importance of Patient Education

It's not enough to prescribe. We need to empower.

We explain:

- Treatment timelines: Pigment takes time to fade
- Consistency is key: Skipping sunscreen or bouncing between products delays results
- The emotional journey: Progress isn't always linear, but we're in it together

By managing expectations and celebrating small wins, we help our patients reclaim confidence, one clear patch at a time.

From Reactive to Proactive

In aesthetic medicine, our role is shifting. We're not just reacting to breakouts, we're preventing them. We're helping patients of color see their skin as worthy of specialized care, not just a footnote in someone else's protocol. And when we treat acne and PIH holistically, with knowledge, intention, and cultural awareness, we don't just change skin. We change lives.

Chapter 19: Melasma. Pathophysiology and Management: Managing One of the Most Stubborn Pigmentary Conditions with Skill, Sensitivity, and Strategy

Melasma is one of the most frustrating skin conditions for both patients and practitioners. It's chronic, recurrent, and emotionally draining. For patients of color, especially women, it often feels like an invisible burden. And yet, we can't let that discourage us. We approach melasma with clinical precision, cultural sensitivity, and the kind of hope that comes from knowing the science.

What Is Melasma?

Melasma is a pigmentary disorder characterized by symmetrical patches of brown or gray-brown discoloration, usually on the face, cheeks, forehead, upper lip, and jawline.

What makes it different from PIH? Melasma is hormonally driven and chronic, with no clear inflammatory trigger and a deeper dermal component that makes it more resistant to treatment.

Who's Affected?

We typically see melasma in:

- Women aged 20–50 (especially in outdoor athletes, during pregnancy, birth control use, or hormonal fluctuations)
- People with darker skin tones
- Patients with a family history of pigment disorders
- Individuals with chronic sun exposure or heat exposure
- Those dealing with stress, thyroid disorders, or photosensitizing medications

The Pathophysiology: Why It's So Complex

Melasma is a multifactorial problem. It involves:

- Melanocyte hyperactivity: Melanocytes are triggered to produce excessive melanin
- Vascular components: There may be increased blood vessels in affected areas
- Disrupted skin barrier: Often worsens due to inappropriate skincare or procedures
- Hormonal influences: Estrogen and progesterone can upregulate pigment production
- UV and visible light exposure: These are major triggers for flares, with visible light impacting SOC patients more intensely

We're not just dealing with surface pigment, we're dealing with epidermal, dermal, and mixed-depth pigmentation that relapses with the slightest provocation.

Assessment and Diagnosis

We start with:

- History: Onset, triggers (pregnancy, new medications), family history, sun exposure
- Skin phototype
- Wood's lamp: Can help distinguish epidermal vs. dermal involvement
- Photography: Baseline documentation for progress tracking

And most importantly, we listen. Patients often come in defeated, feeling dismissed, judged, or told they're imagining it. We validate their concerns and reassure them: "You're not alone, and there are tools that can help."

Treatment Goals: Gentle, Steady, and Sustained

There's no cure, but that doesn't mean there's no hope. Our job is to lighten, prevent recurrence, encourage preventative practices, and support skin health long-term.

First-Line Treatments

- Tinted broad-spectrum sunscreen (SPF 50+): Physical blockers with iron oxide to protect against visible light
- Topical tyrosinase inhibitors: Hydroquinone (short-term), azelaic acid, tranexamic acid, kojic acid, arbutin
- Topical retinoids: Promote cell turnover (adapalene, tretinoin—carefully titrated)
- Triple combination creams: Hydroquinone + retinoid + steroid (used for limited periods)

Procedural Support (Only When Stable)

- Chemical peels: Superficial peels like glycolic, salicylic, or mandelic acid can help but require caution
- Microneedling: May improve pigment over time with the right protocol
- Laser therapy: Low-fluence Q-switched Nd:YAG (1064 nm) in experienced hands only; never first-line

Oral Therapy

- Oral tranexamic acid: Emerging evidence supports its use in refractory melasma. Monitor for thrombotic risk.

The Long Game: Melasma Maintenance

Melasma management is not a 4-week plan. It's a lifestyle and we help our patients understand:

- Flares will happen. That doesn't mean they've failed.
- Skincare consistency > short bursts of treatment.
- Emotional support and aesthetic results go hand in hand.

We set realistic expectations, recommend simple regimens, and schedule follow-ups to adjust and support as needed. Education becomes our most powerful tool.

Cultural Literacy in Melasma Care

We must understand the cultural contexts in which melasma shows up. For many patients of color, skin discoloration isn't "just cosmetic," it's tied to how they're perceived socially and professionally. Our role is to affirm their experiences and offer real strategies, not judgment or vague reassurances.

We don't promise perfect skin. We promise partnership.

Wrapping It All Together

Melasma may be one of the most persistent pigmentary challenges we'll face, but we're not powerless. With the right blend of science, art, and empathy, we help our patients regain control.

Chapter 20: Alopecia and Scalp Concerns

Hair is more than a style, it's tied to culture, identity, health, and confidence. When our patients walk into the exam room concerned about hair loss, they're not just looking for a diagnosis. They're often carrying emotional weight, cultural expectations, and years of frustration. As aesthetic Nurse Practitioners, we have an opportunity to be a trusted guide, someone who listens, educates, and offers real, evidence-based options.

The Most Common Hair Loss Patterns We'll See

We need to be prepared to evaluate and manage the most frequently encountered types of alopecia, especially in patients with richly pigmented skin.

Here are the ones we'll see most often:

- **Traction Alopecia**: Chronic pulling from hairstyles like braids, weaves, buns, or locs can lead to inflammation and eventually scarring, especially along the frontal hairline. Education is key here: early detection and protective styling can help prevent permanent loss.
- **Central Centrifugal Cicatricial Alopecia (CCCA)**: This scarring form of alopecia is especially common among Black women. It often starts at the crown and spreads outward. The challenge? It's usually misdiagnosed or dismissed. We must understand the signs, scaling, tenderness, broken hairs, inflammation, and refer or treat early to preserve the follicles. Evidence shows the damage likely starts during adolescence. Therefore, the recommendation is to start screening around 12 years and older (George et al., 2023).
- **Androgenetic Alopecia**: Also known as female-pattern hair loss, this shows up as diffuse thinning at the crown and top of the scalp. In our patients of color, this may be harder to recognize initially, but it's just as distressing and treatable.

- **Telogen Effluvium:** Acute shedding triggered by stress, illness, childbirth, or even crash diets. It's reversible, but only when we educate patients about the cycle and address the root cause.
- **Alopecia Areata**: An autoimmune condition that causes sudden, round patches of hair loss. It requires both a clinical and compassionate approach since recurrence is common and unpredictable.

Building a Thoughtful Evaluation

When someone comes to us with hair loss, our evaluation goes beyond the scalp:

- What's their styling history?
- Are there signs of inflammation, scarring, or tenderness?
- What medications, stressors, or nutritional changes might be contributing?
- How long has it been going on, and how quickly did it start?
- What does hair loss mean to them, culturally and personally?

We examine the scalp, photograph baseline progress, and, when needed, order labs to evaluate iron levels, thyroid function, or hormones. We may even perform a gentle pull test or scalp biopsy in persistent or unclear cases.

Treatment Must Be Individualized

There is no one-size-fits-all solution for alopecia. That's why we blend clinical judgment with cultural awareness when building treatment plans. Options include:

- Topical treatments: Minoxidil, corticosteroids, or growth-stimulating compounds.
- Oral options: Spironolactone, finasteride, iron supplementation, pumpkin seed oil supplements, or newer therapies like JAK inhibitors for alopecia areata.

- Procedural interventions: PRP (Platelet-Rich Plasma), microneedling with growth factors, and in some cases, low-level laser therapy.
- Lifestyle modifications: Gentle handling, reducing heat and tension, and scalp massage to improve circulation.
- We also talk openly about timelines, hair grows slowly, and most regrowth plans take 3 to 6 months to show meaningful results.

Empowering Through Education
When we approach alopecia with clinical skill and cultural sensitivity, we do more than regrow hair, we restore hope. We break through the silence that often surrounds hair loss in communities of color. We empower our patients with language, tools, and realistic expectations.

This chapter reminds us that hair care is health care. And in our role, we can make a lasting impact on how our patients feel about themselves—inside and out.

Chapter 21: Hair Removal in Skin of Color

Hair removal is one of the most requested aesthetic services and one of the most misunderstood when it comes to richly pigmented skin. We've all seen the marketing: sleek lasers, "painless" treatments, flawless results. But behind the buzzwords is a truth we can't ignore: skin of color requires a different level of clinical knowledge, skill, and cultural sensitivity.

As aesthetic Nurse Practitioners, we must not only master the science of hair removal—we must understand the unique concerns our diverse patients bring into the room.

Understanding the Science (and the Risks)

Hair removal technologies, especially laser hair removal, work by targeting melanin. That's where things get tricky. In skin of color, there's more melanin in both the hair and the epidermis. If we're not careful, lasers meant to destroy hair can also damage the surrounding skin, leading to hyperpigmentation, hypopigmentation, burns, or scarring.

We avoid this by choosing the right wavelengths and settings. For darker skin tones, we prioritize longer wavelengths like:

- Nd:YAG (1064 nm): The gold standard for safety in richly pigmented skin due to deeper penetration and lower melanin absorption in the epidermis.
- Diode (810 nm): Can be safe for moderate skin tones with proper settings and cooling mechanisms.

We also adjust fluence, pulse duration, and cooling to reduce the risk of thermal injury.

Cultural Awareness Matters

Hair removal isn't just cosmetic, it's deeply personal. In some cultures, visible facial hair in women is stigmatized, leading to shame, social withdrawal, or aggressive hair removal practices like plucking or depilatory creams, which can worsen inflammation or pigmentation.

When we understand the cultural context, we can approach consultations with more empathy and build treatment plans that honor both clinical safety and personal goals.

Key Considerations Before Treatment

- Pre-treatment protocols: We ensure patients avoid sun exposure, self-tanners, and certain topicals before their sessions.
- Skin typing: We assess not only the skin phototype but also the presence of melasma, post-inflammatory hyperpigmentation (PIH), or a history of keloids.
- Informed consent: We talk honestly about risks, expected results, and the need for multiple sessions, usually 6 to 8 sessions spaced 4 to 6 weeks apart.
- Patch testing: Especially critical for skin of color. A small test area helps us assess skin response before committing to full treatment.

Post-Treatment Care and PIH Prevention

Post-laser inflammation can trigger pigment changes in darker skin, so we don't skip aftercare:

- Cooling gels and anti-inflammatory topicals
- Avoidance of sun exposure and heat for at least 48 hours
- Gentle cleansers and barrier repair
- Short-term use of topical steroids if needed

We may also pre-treat or follow-up with pigment inhibitors like azelaic acid or kojic acid to minimize PIH.

Building Trust and Long-Term Results

When done right, hair removal can be transformative. Our patients deserve not only smoother skin but also safer, smarter options. We're not just reducing hair, we're reducing harm, fear, and misinformation.

This is where our expertise shines. We don't just follow protocols, we tailor care, ask deeper questions, and offer results that respect both biology and identity.

Chapter 22: Hypertrophic Scars and Keloids: Prevention, treatment modalities, and how to counsel patients predisposed to these scarring patterns

When we step into the world of aesthetics, we quickly realize that the skin tells stories far deeper than surface-level texture or tone. Hypertrophic scars and keloids are among the most emotionally and physically complex narratives our patients may carry. As aesthetic Nurse Practitioners, it's our responsibility to understand not only the clinical presentation of these scars but also the cultural, genetic, and psychosocial layers that shape how patients experience them.

Understanding the Differences

Hypertrophic scars and keloids are often grouped together, but they differ significantly. Hypertrophic scars stay confined to the original wound site and may improve over time. Keloids, on the other hand, grow beyond the wound boundary and rarely regress without intervention. Both can result from trauma, surgical procedures, piercings, acne, burns, or even minor skin injuries, and both are more prevalent in patients with richly pigmented skin.

Our clinical approach begins with this differentiation. When we can confidently identify whether we're dealing with a hypertrophic scar or a keloid, we can better educate our patients, manage expectations, and select an appropriate treatment pathway.

Cultural Sensitivity in Scar Conversations

Scars carry cultural meaning. In some communities, keloids are seen as family traits passed from generation to generation, normalized, and even accepted. In others, they may cause deep distress, especially if the scarring affects highly visible areas such as the face, neck, chest, or ears. We must approach these conversations with cultural sensitivity, avoiding language that pathologizes or diminishes the patient's lived experience. Patients may come to us unsure whether they want treatment or simply want to understand their options. Let's be the provider who listens, validates, and co-creates the care plan. That's the kind of aesthetic practice that builds trust and changes lives.

Prevention Strategies

When it comes to keloid-prone patients, prevention is our best tool. That starts during the consultation process. We should always ask about a personal or family history of keloids or hypertrophic scarring. If the patient has a history, we must weigh the risks of elective aesthetic procedures, especially injectables, piercings, or surgical excisions, with a preventive lens.

Strategies we may consider include:

- Avoiding elective skin trauma in high-risk individuals
- Using silicone gel sheets or pressure therapy post-procedure
- Incorporating intralesional corticosteroids at the first sign of abnormal scar formation
- Pre-procedure patient education on wound care, sun protection, and signs of abnormal healing

Treatment Modalities

There is no one-size-fits-all protocol for scar management. We must blend evidence-based approaches with individualized care.

Common treatments include:

- Intralesional corticosteroid injections – Often first-line for reducing inflammation and flattening raised tissue
- Silicone-based products – Including sheets and gels, used consistently over several months
- Cryotherapy – Especially effective for small keloids, though pigmentary changes are a concern in skin of color
- Laser therapy – Pulsed dye laser (PDL) can help reduce redness and texture, but it must be used cautiously
- Surgical excision – Only with adjunct therapies to prevent recurrence, such as radiation, steroids, or pressure garments
- Emerging treatments – Topical imiquimod, 5-fluorouracil, and combination therapies are showing promise

As we offer these treatments, let's remain mindful of our patient's skin type, lifestyle, and treatment goals. Our aim is not just to improve appearance, but to reduce discomfort, enhance confidence, and restore agency.

Counseling and Long-Term Support

These scars may be persistent, and so must we. Follow-up is key. Your treatment recommendations should be proactive, not reactive. Encourage patients to track changes, take photos, and stay engaged with their treatment regimen. And just as important, normalize their experience. Keloids and hypertrophic scars are not failures of healing; they are expressions of a unique biological response. When we frame it this way, we empower our patients to see their skin not as flawed, but as resilient.

Chapter 23: Periorbital Rejuvenation: Learn to evaluate and treat the delicate under-eye area, including common complaints and non-surgical options.

The eyes may be the window to the soul, but in aesthetics, they're also the first place many of our patients point to when they say, "I look tired all the time." Periorbital rejuvenation is more than brightening under-eye circles, it's about restoring vitality, balance, and expression to the face in a way that feels natural and empowering.

The Importance of a Thoughtful Approach

The periorbital area is a high-stakes zone. The skin here is thin, the anatomy is complex, and even minor enhancements can make a dramatic impact, for better or worse. That's why we must combine clinical precision with a highly individualized, culturally sensitive approach.

No two patients age the same way. Factors like volume loss, hyperpigmentation, skin laxity, and lifestyle habits all play a role. And for patients with richly pigmented skin, we must approach pigmentary changes with extra care to avoid exacerbating concerns like postinflammatory hyperpigmentation or uneven tone.

Common Concerns We See

When patients seek periorbital treatment, they often use words like "tired," "sunken," "puffy," or "dark." Our job is to translate those concerns into clinical terms:

- Volume Loss – Creates hollowness and tear troughs
- Pigmentation – May be due to genetics, vascular congestion, or lifestyle factors like sleep and stress
- Laxity – Sagging of the eyelids or undereye area
- Edema or Puffiness – Sometimes from fat herniation or lymphatic stagnation
- Fine Lines and Wrinkles – From years of expression and UV exposure

During our consultation, we should always ask what specifically bothers the patient and when they notice it most. Does the puffiness fluctuate? Are they wearing more makeup to cover discoloration? Do they feel their appearance affects how others perceive them? This insight shapes our plan.

Non-Surgical Options in Our Toolkit
Here's where we shine as aesthetic NPs: offering results-driven, non-invasive solutions backed by both science and artistry:

- Topical Skincare – Ingredients like caffeine, peptides, vitamin C, and niacinamide can improve pigmentation and puffiness with consistent use
- Chemical Peels – Carefully selected superficial peels can help with pigment concerns, especially when combined with home care
- Microneedling – With or without PRP, this can improve skin texture and firmness while respecting the thin skin of the periorbital area
- Neuromodulators – Targeting the orbicularis oculi can soften crow's feet and subtly lift the brow
- EZ Gel PRF – A natural biostimulator made from your own blood, EZ Gel uses platelet-rich fibrin to smooth fine lines, improve skin tone, and stimulate collagen all while being gentle enough for delicate areas like under the eyes.

- Dermal Fillers – When placed with precision and caution in the tear trough area, fillers can reduce shadows and restore a youthful contour
- Laser and Light-Based Devices – Fractionated lasers or radiofrequency microneedling (when used with cultural awareness) can improve tone and tightness

We must always assess for contraindications, especially in patients with skin of color. Start conservative, and monitor for any signs of hyperpigmentation or prolonged erythema. Less is often more.

Guiding the Patient Journey
Patients may come in with screenshots, filter-heavy selfies, or unrealistic expectations. Let's anchor them in what's achievable and sustainable.

We can say things like:
"Let's focus on brightening and hydrating the area first, then reassess in 6 weeks."

"We'll go slow with filler here, just enough to refresh without looking 'done.'"

We're not chasing perfection. We're co-creating a version of themselves that feels confident, rested, and authentic.

Final Thoughts
Periorbital rejuvenation requires patience, precision, and presence. As aesthetic NPs, we don't just restore volume, we restore light, connection, and confidence. This work, especially around the eyes, invites us to honor both the science of aging and the stories our patients carry with them.

PART V: TREATMENT MODALITIES & TECHNIQUES

- **Facial Rejuvenation and Contouring**
  - Holistic strategies to address volume loss, skin laxity, and facial harmony using injectables and other non-invasive tools.

- **Neuromodulators: Botox & Beyond**
  - Mechanisms of action, dosing considerations, and patient education for wrinkle reduction and therapeutic uses.

- **Soft Tissue Augmentation (Fillers)**
  - Safety-first techniques for enhancing lips, cheeks, and jawlines with hyaluronic acid and other filler products.

- **Laser and Light-Based Devices in Diverse Skin Tones**
  - This chapter provides critical insight into choosing safe energy-based modalities for darker skin tones

- **Surgical Treatment Options**
  - An overview of minor and major procedures often integrated with non-surgical care, including when to refer.

PART V: TREATMENT MODALITIES & TECHNIQUES

- **Topical Treatments for Aesthetic Conditions**
    - Prescribed and OTC options for pigmentation, aging, and texture—with product examples and application protocols.

Chapter 24: Facial Rejuvenation and Contouring: Restoring Harmony and Confidence Through Non-Surgical Aesthetics

As aesthetic nurse practitioners, we often meet patients who look in the mirror and no longer recognize the reflection staring back at them. It's not just about wrinkles or sagging skin, it's about identity, confidence, and feeling aligned with one's best self. Facial rejuvenation and contouring go beyond simple "anti-aging" techniques. We're working holistically to restore harmony, enhance natural features, and help our patients feel radiant from the inside out.

A Holistic Approach to the Aging Face

Facial aging is a three-dimensional process involving bone resorption, fat pad descent, muscle laxity, and skin texture changes. That means we can't treat a nasolabial fold in isolation or fill a cheek without considering the temple hollowing or jawline contour. Each feature is part of a bigger picture, our job is to step back, assess globally, and build a strategy that restores balance, proportion, and youthful energy.

Our Toolkit for Transformation

Our non-surgical options are powerful when used with precision. Hyaluronic acid fillers help us replace lost volume, recontour the midface, and restore support. Neuromodulators smooth dynamic wrinkles and elevate features like the brow. Biostimulatory agents like Sculptra or Radiesse improve skin quality and subtly lift over time. Energy-based devices like radiofrequency and ultrasound can improve collagen and skin tightness without downtime. When we combine these strategically, we create results that are natural, elegant, and personalized.

Listening to the Face—and the Patient

Facial rejuvenation isn't just technical. We must understand how our patients perceive their own aging, how cultural and personal identity plays into their goals, and what their unique anatomy requires. For some, the goal is refreshment; for others, it's enhancement. It's not one-size-fits-all. We listen, we educate, and we invite our clients to participate using shared-decision making.

The Power of Incremental Change

We don't have to "fix" everything in one visit. Sometimes, the best outcomes come from layering treatments over time. A touch here, a lift there, this approach not only protects safety but also builds trust and gives the patient time to adjust to their evolving appearance.

Redefining What It Means to Age Gracefully

In aesthetic nursing, we're not trying to erase age. We're embracing it while giving our patients tools to feel empowered and refreshed. Our work isn't about chasing trends, it's about helping people look like the best version of themselves, at every stage of life.

Chapter 25: Neuromodulators: Botox & Beyond: Relax, Rejuvenate, and Reclaim Confidence

Let's talk neuromodulators, the powerhouse tools in our aesthetic practice that help soften expression lines, refine facial contours, and support both cosmetic and therapeutic outcomes. From the classic "Botox®" to newer formulations like Xeomin®, Dysport®, Daxxify™, and Jeuveau®, we're working with refined agents that temporarily relax targeted muscles while preserving natural movement.

Understanding the Science

Neuromodulators are purified botulinum toxin type A proteins that inhibit the release of acetylcholine at the neuromuscular junction, temporarily preventing muscle contraction. In aesthetic medicine, this translates into softened glabellar lines (frown lines or "11 lines"), smoothed crow's feet, elevated brows, and even jawline slimming. It's subtle science with powerful effects; when dosed and placed correctly, the results can look seamless.

Dosing with Intention

Each patient brings unique anatomy, muscle strength, and aesthetic goals. Dosing should reflect that. A patient with strong frontalis activity (raise the eyebrows and wrinkle the forehead) may require more product for the forehead than someone with thinner, less active muscles. The key is to tailor each treatment plan based on a comprehensive facial assessment and patient preferences, not a one-size-fits-all map.

Beyond Wrinkle Reduction

Neuromodulators aren't just for frown lines. We use them to treat masseter hypertrophy, reduce platysmal banding, lift the nasal tip, treat gummy smiles, and ease tension in the trapezius muscles, the "trap tox" trend, which blends aesthetic and functional outcomes. Therapeutically, we may see off-label use in chronic migraines, hyperhidrosis, and bruxism, areas where our scope of practice and state regulations allow.

Educating Patients on Expectations

Patient education is everything. We set expectations about onset (typically 3–5 days), peak effect (around 2 weeks), and duration (3–4 months for most products). We discuss potential side effects, such as brow heaviness, ptosis, or asymmetry, and how these can be minimized through careful technique. Transparency builds trust, and trust keeps our patients coming back.

Keeping It Natural

We've all seen, or heard about, the overdone forehead or frozen smile. Our job is to dispel the myths and show that neuromodulators can enhance without erasing expression. It's about precision, not paralysis. By preserving some dynamic movement, we keep our patients looking like themselves, just more rested, refreshed, and refined.

A Subtle Art with a Big Impact

As nurse practitioners, we approach neuromodulators with clinical insight and aesthetic sensitivity. These treatments may seem simple on the surface, but they require anatomical mastery, a deep understanding of facial dynamics, and the ability to translate patient goals into thoughtful, safe interventions.

Neuromodulators Vocabulary List

1. Neuromodulators

Agents that modify nerve activity by altering the transmission of signals between neurons. In aesthetics, they refer to substances like botulinum toxin that reduce muscle activity to soften wrinkles and alter facial contours.

2. Botulinum Toxin Type A

A purified neurotoxin derived from Clostridium botulinum bacteria. Used in small, controlled doses to temporarily paralyze muscles for cosmetic and therapeutic effects. The term "neuromodulator" is a broad term referring to substances that influence the activity of neurons, while "neurotoxins" are specifically a type of neuromodulator that disrupts the normal functioning of nerve cells. In the context of cosmetic treatments, neurotoxins like Botox are used to relax muscles and reduce wrinkles.

3. Acetylcholine

A neurotransmitter that facilitates communication between nerves and muscles. Neuromodulators block its release at the neuromuscular junction, preventing muscle contraction.

4. Neuromuscular Junction

The site where a motor neuron communicates with a muscle fiber, triggering contraction. This is the primary target of botulinum toxin in cosmetic use.

5. Glabellar Lines

Vertical lines or “frown lines” that form between the eyebrows, often treated with neuromodulators.

6. Crow's Feet
Fine lines radiating from the outer corners of the eyes, commonly addressed in aesthetic treatments with neuromodulators.

7. Frontalis Muscle
The forehead muscle responsible for raising the eyebrows. It creates horizontal forehead lines when contracted.

8. Masseter Hypertrophy
Enlargement of the masseter muscles (jaw muscles), often due to teeth grinding or clenching (bruxism). Treatable with neuromodulators to slim the lower face.

9. Platysmal Banding
Vertical neck bands that appear due to the contraction of the platysma muscle. These can be softened with neuromodulator injections.

10. Nasal Tip Lift
Aesthetic technique using neuromodulators to relax the muscle that pulls the nasal tip downward, resulting in a more lifted appearance.

11. Gummy Smile
A smile that reveals an excessive amount of gum tissue. Neuromodulators can be used to relax the muscles that elevate the upper lip, reducing gum exposure.

12. Trapezius Muscle (Trap Tox)
Large muscle extending over the back of the neck and shoulders. Injecting neuromodulators here can relieve tension and pain, and aesthetically elongate the neck.

13. Bruxism
Involuntary grinding or clenching of the teeth, often during sleep. Neuromodulators can reduce muscle activity in the jaw to alleviate symptoms.

14. Hyperhidrosis
Excessive sweating, commonly treated by injecting neuromodulators into areas like the underarms to block sweat gland activity.

15. Chronic Migraines
Severe, recurring headaches that can be treated with neuromodulators by targeting specific head and neck muscles to reduce symptom frequency and severity.

16. Off-label Use
Using a drug for an indication not officially approved by regulatory agencies. Common in aesthetic and medical practices where evidence supports safety and efficacy.

17. Dosing
The specific amount of neuromodulator administered. It must be tailored to each patient's muscle strength, anatomy, and goals.

Chapter 26: Soft Tissue Augmentation (Fillers): Volume, Contour, and Confidence—On Our Terms

Dermal fillers allow us to restore youthful contours, smooth lines, and enhance natural features without surgery. But the artistry of filler is so much more than volume, it's about harmony, structure, and intention. As aesthetic nurse practitioners, we blend clinical precision with artistic vision to help our patients feel like the best version of themselves.

Understanding Fillers: What's in the Syringe?

Most fillers used today are made from hyaluronic acid (HA), a naturally occurring substance in the body that attracts water and hydrates the skin. We also have non-HA options like calcium hydroxylapatite (Radiesse®) and poly-L-lactic acid (Sculptra®) that stimulate collagen production for gradual, long-term improvement. Each product serves a different purpose; HA is ideal for sculpting lips and under-eyes, while biostimulatory fillers are better for deeper volume restoration.

The Faces We Treat, The Features We Frame

When we assess a face, we're not just looking at lines or folds, we're evaluating proportion, balance, and symmetry. Whether we're enhancing lips, contouring cheeks, defining the jawline, or filling tear troughs, we consider how each feature works together. Our patients aren't templates, they're individuals with diverse goals and unique beauty standards that guide our treatment recommendations.

Safety First: Anatomy Is Non-Negotiable

Filler complications can be serious, and that's why our approach is grounded in deep anatomical knowledge and safety protocols. We understand vascular danger zones, use aspiration and slow injection techniques when appropriate, and always keep hyaluronidase on hand. Safe injection is not just good practice, it's the foundation of patient trust and professional integrity.

Managing Expectations and Outcomes

We help our patients understand that fillers are not one-and-done solutions. Maintenance is key, as most HA fillers last between 6–18 months depending on the area, product used, and metabolism. We talk about swelling, bruising, and the importance of gradual refinement over time. That transparency helps our patients become informed partners in their aesthetic journey.

Cultural Sensitivity in Facial Augmentation

We approach each treatment through the lens of cultural literacy. Not all lips want to be fuller. Not all jawlines want to be slimmer. What we consider "ideal" in one population may not resonate in another. We honor diverse beauty goals by asking thoughtful questions and listening to what patients see when they look in the mirror.

Creating with Purpose

Filler is a powerful tool, but only when used with purpose. We don't chase trends; we chase confidence, alignment, and authenticity. When patients feel seen, heard, and respected, the results are more than cosmetic.

What is Hyaluronidase?

Hyaluronidase is an enzyme that breaks down hyaluronic acid (HA), a naturally occurring substance in the skin that retains moisture and provides volume. In aesthetic medicine, hyaluronidase is used to dissolve dermal fillers made from hyaluronic acid. It's a precision tool in our clinical arsenal, offering both safety and correction when outcomes don't go as planned or when patient preferences change.

Why We Use It

Whether we're managing overcorrection, asymmetry, migration, or vascular compromise, hyaluronidase allows us to act quickly and confidently. This enzyme essentially "undoes" HA-based filler placement by breaking down the filler particles and allowing the body to reabsorb them. Its applications include:

- Reversing undesirable aesthetic results
- Dissolving migrated filler (e.g., in the lips or tear troughs)
- Managing vascular occlusion (an urgent complication where filler blocks blood flow)
- Softening overfilled areas to restore natural contours

Mechanism of Action

Hyaluronidase works by cleaving the bonds between hyaluronic acid molecules, making them smaller and more water-soluble. This enzymatic activity begins within minutes and continues for several hours. Results can often be seen immediately, although full effects may take up to 24–48 hours.

Types and Formulations

Hyaluronidase is available in several forms, including:

- Vitrase® (ovine-derived)
- Hylenex® (recombinant human; the only FDA-approved recombinant human hyaluronidase)
- Hyalase® (bovine-derived, commonly used outside the U.S.)

It's important to know the origin of the product, especially in patients with allergies to animal proteins.

Dosing and Technique

Dosing depends on the type and amount of filler, depth of placement, and desired degree of correction. We often start conservatively and reassess in follow-up appointments. It's essential to counsel patients that hyaluronidase may also break down natural HA in the skin, potentially causing temporary volume loss or swelling.

Patient Education and Cultural Sensitivity

For many patients, especially those from underrepresented communities, there may be anxiety around "dissolving" treatments. It's our job to provide clear, culturally sensitive education about why hyaluronidase is used, how it works, and what results to expect. Transparency builds trust, especially when reversing a treatment they may have received elsewhere.

Clinical Pearls

- Always do a patch test if you suspect a history of allergies.
- Hyaluronidase is not effective on non-HA fillers like Radiesse® or Sculptra®.
- It's a vital tool in vascular emergency protocols, every injector should have it on hand.

Understanding Dermal Fillers: Composition, Function, and Skin of Color Considerations

As aesthetic nurse practitioners, we know that not all fillers are created equal, and neither are our patients' needs. From enhancing contour to restoring volume, the filler we choose should align with anatomy, skin biology, and individualized aesthetic goals. When treating patients with skin of color, we must also consider melanin-rich skin's tendency toward post-inflammatory hyperpigmentation (PIH), keloids, and textural shifts.

Let's explore the most common filler types used in aesthetic medicine:

1. Hyaluronic Acid (HA) Fillers

Examples: Juvederm®, Restylane®, Belotero Balance®, RHA Collection

Composition: Cross-linked hyaluronic acid, a sugar molecule naturally found in the skin.

Function: Adds volume, hydrates the skin, and enhances facial features. Used for lips, cheeks, tear troughs, nasolabial folds, jawline, and hands.

Advantages:

- Reversible with hyaluronidase
- Immediate results

Wide range of viscosities and flexibility for different anatomical areas

2. Calcium Hydroxylapatite (CaHA)
Example: Radiesse®

Composition: Microspheres suspended in a gel carrier.

Function: Provides structure and stimulates collagen production. Best for deep lines, jawline, cheeks, and nasolabial folds.

Advantages:

- Longer-lasting than HA (12–18 months)
- Collagen stimulation improves skin integrity over time

Considerations for Skin of Color:

- Not reversible—requires precise technique and deep placement to avoid complications.
- Higher risk of nodule formation if injected too superficially.
- May be avoided in areas prone to scarring or in patients with a history of keloids.

3. Poly-L-Lactic Acid (PLLA)
Example: Sculptra®

Composition: A biodegradable synthetic polymer that stimulates collagen production over time.

Function: Gradual volumization and skin thickening, particularly in areas with fat loss (e.g., temples, cheeks).

Advantages:

- Subtle, natural results over several sessions
- Especially useful in HIV-associated lipoatrophy and age-related facial hollowing

Considerations for Skin of Color:

- Risk of papules or nodules if not diluted properly or if massaging instructions are not followed.
- Must counsel patients that results are not immediate, education and expectation management are essential.
- PIH is rare but possible if the injection technique is aggressive or inflammatory.

4. Polymethylmethacrylate (PMMA)

Example: Bellafill®

Composition: Tiny PMMA beads suspended in a collagen gel carrier.

Function: Provides permanent structural support and long-term correction.

Advantages:

- Longest-lasting filler option (5+ years)
- Indicated for acne scarring and deep wrinkles

Considerations for Skin of Color:

- Permanent = higher risk profile
- Not ideal for first-time filler patients or those prone to hypertrophic scarring
- Overcorrection is difficult to fix, so conservative dosing and patient selection are critical

Clinical Considerations for Skin of Color

- Injection Technique Matters: Use blunt-tip cannulas where possible to minimize trauma and bruising. Fewer passes = lower risk of PIH.

- Patient Education: Explain the importance of post-treatment care, especially avoiding sun exposure and using pigment-safe topicals.

- Start Conservatively: A little goes a long way; layering over multiple sessions can achieve natural results while reducing inflammatory risk.

- Know Your Products: HA fillers are safest in melanated skin, particularly for first-time treatments. Use reversible products until you understand each patient's tissue response.

Chapter 27: Laser and Light-Based Devices in Diverse Skin Tones

When it comes to aesthetic dermatology, lasers and light-based technologies are game-changers, but in diverse skin tones, they're not without risk. As nurse practitioners, we are entrusted with the responsibility to deliver safe, effective, and inclusive care. That means understanding the science behind how light interacts with melanin, being intentional with device selection, and mastering protocols that reduce adverse outcomes in richly pigmented skin.

The Physics of Light and Skin

Laser and light-based therapies work through selective photothermolysis, targeting specific chromophores (like melanin, hemoglobin, or water) with precise wavelengths of light to achieve a therapeutic effect. In lighter skin tones, there's a wide margin for error, but in darker skin types, the stakes are higher. Melanin, abundant in deeper complexions, absorbs a broad spectrum of light. Without proper precautions, this can lead to burns, post-inflammatory hyperpigmentation (PIH), hypopigmentation, and scarring.

The Importance of Cultural Awareness in Device Selection

Cultural sensitivity in aesthetic care goes beyond language, it's embedded in the treatment planning process. The lasers and light-based devices we choose must be tailored to the patient's skin biology and aesthetic goals.

For example:

- Nd:YAG 1064 nm is the gold standard for hair removal and vascular lesions in darker skin due to its deeper penetration and minimal melanin absorption.

- Non-ablative fractional lasers (such as the 1550 nm erbium glass) are preferred for texture and scarring without excessive downtime or pigment disruption.
- Intense Pulsed Light (IPL) is often contraindicated in darker skin due to its broad-spectrum wavelengths and melanin attraction.

Patient Assessment: The Foundation of Safety

Before initiating any energy-based treatment, a comprehensive skin assessment is critical. This includes evaluating the patient's:

- Skin phototype
- History of PIH or hypertrophic and keloid formation
- Current skincare routine and medication use
- Recent sun exposure or tanning
- Expectations and cultural influences on beauty

This evaluation isn't just clinical, it's culturally literate. Many patients of color may have concerns about pigment alteration, delayed healing, or historical mistrust of lasers. Our role is to create a psychologically safe environment where patients feel informed, heard, and empowered.

Pre- and Post-Treatment Protocols

Protocol matters, especially for patients with skin of color. We prepare the skin with melanin-safe topicals (like hydroquinone alternatives or antioxidants) and may recommend gentle pre-treatment regimens to reduce inflammation. Post-treatment, we stress sun avoidance, use of physical blockers (like zinc-based SPF), and barrier-repairing products. For PIH-prone patients, early intervention with agents like azelaic acid, tranexamic acid, or topical retinoids can mitigate risk.

Clinical Pearls and Pitfalls

- Test spots should always be performed when working with new patients or devices.
- Avoid treating inflamed or compromised skin.
- Education is everything—patients need realistic expectations about how many treatments are required and what results to anticipate.
- Lower fluence and increased pulse durations can minimize thermal injury in melanin-rich skin.
    - In melanin-rich skin, there is a greater risk of thermal injury during laser procedures due to the increased absorption of energy by epidermal melanin. To reduce this risk, providers can adjust laser settings by lowering the fluence (energy per unit area) and increasing the pulse duration (the time over which energy is delivered). Lower fluence decreases the overall energy delivered, while longer pulse durations allow heat to disperse more gradually. This combination minimizes peak thermal exposure to the skin's surface while still effectively targeting deeper structures such as hair follicles or pigmented lesions. These adjustments are essential for providing safe and effective laser treatments in patients with darker skin tones.

Championing Representation in Laser Education

Historically, skin of color has been underrepresented in device research and clinical training. As aesthetic nurse practitioners, we must challenge this gap by advocating for inclusive clinical trials, diverse before-and-after imagery, and continued education in multicultural dermatology. Cultural literacy is a clinical competency and when we apply it to energy-based treatments, we don't just prevent harm; we build trust and change lives.

Chapter 28: Surgical Treatment Options

While non-invasive aesthetic interventions have revolutionized the way we restore and rejuvenate the face and body, there remains an important role for surgical treatments in comprehensive aesthetic care. As nurse practitioners, understanding surgical options, even if we do not perform them ourselves, elevates our ability to educate, counsel, and refer patients confidently.

This chapter is about more than procedures. It's about knowing when non-invasive isn't enough, recognizing surgical synergy, and being a trusted guide along our patients' aesthetic journeys.

Surgical Integration in Aesthetic Practice

Surgical and non-surgical interventions aren't opposites; they're complementary. Whether we're treating moderate to severe skin laxity, congenital anomalies, or volume loss that non-injectables can't adequately address, surgery often becomes the next logical step.

Understanding these options allows us to:

- Refer appropriately and build cross-disciplinary relationships
- Set realistic expectations for outcomes and timelines
- Integrate post-op aesthetic treatments for maintenance

Common Surgical Procedures and Their Indications

Blepharoplasty (Eyelid Surgery)

- Purpose: Removes excess skin and fat from the upper and/or lower eyelids.
- Candidates: Patients with hooded eyes, under-eye bags, or vision obstruction.
- NP Role: Recognize when periorbital volume loss or skin redundancy surpasses the reach of fillers or neurotoxins.

Rhytidectomy (Facelift)

- Purpose: Lifts and tightens facial tissues, reduces sagging, and smooths deep wrinkles.
- Candidates: Patients with advanced aging or volume loss not responding to fillers/threads.
- NP Role: Provide adjunctive treatments post-surgery (e.g., skin quality boosters, neuromodulators).

Neck Lift / Submental Liposuction

- Purpose: Tightens loose neck skin and removes excess fat.
- Candidates: Patients with prominent neck bands, jowls, or double chins.
- NP Role: Educate on alternatives (e.g., Kybella®, RF microneedling) and explain long-term benefits of surgery.

Brow Lift

- Purpose: Elevates sagging eyebrows and reduces forehead lines.
- Candidates: Patients with drooping brows that give a tired or angry appearance.
- NP Role: Distinguish between ptosis and brow heaviness; discuss how Botox® can offer temporary lift vs. surgical permanence.

Fat Transfer

- Purpose: Transplants autologous fat (fat harvested from one part of the patient's body to another) from body to face or other areas.
- Candidates: Patients seeking natural, long-lasting volume restoration.
- NP Role: Discuss pros/cons vs. fillers, including potential for fat survival variability.

Body Contouring Surgeries
Includes:

- Abdominoplasty (Tummy Tuck)
- Liposuction
- Gluteal Augmentation (BBL)
- Thigh and Arm Lifts

These procedures reshape the body following weight loss or pregnancy and are often combined with non-surgical skin tightening or cellulite treatments.

Abdominoplasty (Tummy Tuck)
Purpose:
Removes excess abdominal skin and fat while tightening weakened abdominal muscles to create a firmer, smoother abdomen.

Who It's For:
Often performed after pregnancy or significant weight loss. Ideal candidates are at a stable weight and have realistic expectations.

Key Considerations:

- Patients with darker skin tones may have a higher risk for hyperpigmentation or keloid formation at incision sites.
- Compression garments and scar management should be discussed early to support healing and minimize complications.
- Important to counsel on smoking cessation and medical optimization before surgery.

Liposuction

Purpose:

Surgical fat removal using suction. Common areas include the abdomen, flanks, thighs, arms, and chin.

Who It's For:

Not a weight-loss procedure but great for stubborn fat resistant to diet and exercise.

Key Considerations:

- Results can be enhanced and maintained with body contouring devices like radiofrequency or ultrasound-based treatments.
- In skin of color, post-inflammatory hyperpigmentation (PIH) or hypopigmentation at incision sites is a potential concern.
- Irregular fat removal can lead to contour deformities; precise technique and post-op care matter.

Gluteal Augmentation (Brazilian Butt Lift or BBL)

Purpose:

Fat is harvested via liposuction from one area (usually the abdomen or thighs) and injected into the gluteal region for volume and shape.

Who It's For:

Individuals seeking enhanced buttock volume and contour without implants.

Key Considerations:

- One of the most controversial and high-risk aesthetic procedures due to risk of fat embolism if improperly performed.

- Educate patients on safety protocols, board-certified surgeons, and realistic outcomes.
- In skin of color, extra attention is needed to avoid pigment changes or scarring from both liposuction and fat grafting sites.

Thigh and Arm Lifts (Thighplasty and Brachioplasty)
Purpose:
Removes sagging skin and fat from the inner thighs or upper arms; often needed after major weight loss.

Who It's For:
Patients experiencing skin laxity that doesn't respond to non-surgical tightening treatments.

Key Considerations:

- Incisions are typically long and in visible areas; set clear expectations about scar placement and healing.
- As with other excisional surgeries, there's a greater likelihood of hypertrophic scarring in patients with richly pigmented skin.
- Post-op care includes scar massage, silicone sheets, and sometimes laser therapy to optimize scar outcomes.

Surgical Considerations for Skin of Color
Melanin-rich skin requires a nuanced approach. We must be culturally sensitive and clinically informed.

Keloid and Hypertrophic Scar Risk

- Patients with deeper skin types are at increased risk for abnormal scarring. Surgeons should use tension-reducing techniques and post-op silicone protocols. As NPs, we can educate patients on scar prevention, offer post-op scar management, and screen for personal or family history.

Pigmentation Changes

- Post-surgical PIH or hypopigmentation is more likely in patients with skin of color, particularly after ablative laser treatments or aggressive resurfacing. Counseling and SPF compliance are critical.

Cultural Literacy in Aesthetic Preferences

- Facial balance, beauty standards, and surgical goals vary significantly. Listen deeply, never assume, and tailor your counseling with cultural awareness and respect for identity and beauty ideals.

Our Role: Advocate, Educator, Collaborator

Even if we don't hold the scalpel, we are an essential part of the patient's care team. We prepare them, walk beside them, and help them maintain and enhance results. Whether it's combining neuromodulators post-facelift or guiding a patient toward a reputable plastic surgeon, our clinical judgment and communication bridge the gap between surgery and confidence. Surgical treatment options aren't the end of a journey, they're a next chapter. And we're ready to lead our patients there with clarity, care, and skill.

Chapter 29: Topical Treatments for Aesthetic Conditions: Prescribed and OTC options for pigmentation, aging, and texture

In aesthetics, topical treatments are often the unsung heroes. They bridge in-clinic procedures and daily skin health maintenance, giving us powerful tools to address pigmentation, aging, and texture non-invasively. Whether we're complementing laser and injectable treatments or designing a routine for patients new to aesthetics, our ability to prescribe, recommend, and educate on topical therapies directly influences outcomes.

Pigmentation: Targeted Lightening with Sensitivity
Hyperpigmentation, including melasma, postinflammatory hyperpigmentation (PIH), and sun-induced dark spots, remains a top concern, particularly in skin of color. Our approach must balance efficacy with caution to prevent irritation and rebound pigment.

Key Ingredients:

- Hydroquinone (2–4%) – Gold standard for short-term use; monitor for signs of ochronosis or rebound effects. *Experienced dermatologists and dermatology NPs may use a higher concentration.
- Tranexamic Acid – Oral and topical forms are gaining traction for melasma and diffuse discoloration.
- Kojic Acid, Arbutin, Licorice Extract – Gentler botanical lighteners suitable for long-term use and sensitive skin.
- Azelaic Acid (15–20%) – Antimicrobial, anti-inflammatory, and pigment-suppressing; excellent for acne-related PIH.
- Tretinoin or Retinol – Promotes cell turnover, fading discoloration gradually.

Protocol Tip: Start with alternate-day application for patients with richly pigmented skin to minimize irritation. Always include Tinted SPF in the regimen; topicals are ineffective without sun protection.

Aging: Barrier Repair and Cellular Renewal

Aging is multifactorial, with collagen breakdown, decreased elasticity, dullness, and fine lines. Topical regimens should be customized based on the patient's age, skin type, and other procedures being performed.

Core Components:

- Retinoids (Tretinoin, Adapalene, Retinaldehyde) – Stimulate collagen, smooth texture, and even skin tone.
- Peptides – Support skin repair and boost elasticity.
- Antioxidants (Vitamin C, E, Ferulic Acid, Resveratrol) – Neutralize oxidative stress, brighten skin.
- Niacinamide – A versatile favorite for improving elasticity, fading pigmentation, and enhancing barrier function.
- Growth Factors – Aid in healing and rejuvenation post-procedures.

Product Example

Patients undergoing microneedling or laser treatments benefit from post-procedure kits with gentle cleansers, barrier creams, and growth factor serums.

Texture: Smoother Skin Without Aggression

Patients seeking smooth, glassy skin often battle with rough patches, enlarged pores, or acne-related scarring. Gentle exfoliation and hydration are key, especially for melanated skin prone to PIH.

Effective Ingredients:

- Alpha Hydroxy Acids (Glycolic, Lactic Acid) – Chemical exfoliation for fine lines and dullness.
- Beta Hydroxy Acid (Salicylic Acid) – Ideal for acne-prone and oily skin.
- Polyhydroxy Acids (PHAs) – Less irritating, perfect for sensitive skin and patients with eczema or rosacea.
- Urea & Lactic Acid (in lower concentrations) – Excellent for rough body skin and keratosis pilaris.

Application Protocol: Introduce exfoliants gradually. Pair with moisturizers containing ceramides or hyaluronic acid to maintain barrier integrity.

Patient Education: Making It Stick

Even the best treatment plan fails without proper use. We must coach patients on:

- Product layering (thinnest to thickest)
- Patch testing before introducing actives
- Consistent SPF (daily, broad-spectrum, Tinted SPF 50+)
- When to pause actives before and after procedures

Creating easy-to-follow skincare instructions, printed handouts, or digital guides adds value and improves adherence.

OTC vs. Prescription: Know When to Step In

While many OTC options offer strong benefits, some patients require prescription-strength actives to see meaningful results. The decision should be based on severity, duration, prior product use, and skin sensitivity.

As aesthetic NPs, our expertise allows us to demystify the skincare market, cut through marketing noise, and deliver high-impact, personalized care. Topicals aren't just the "before and after," they are the during, the foundation that supports lasting results and patient confidence.

PART VI: BUSINESS, RESEARCH, AND EDUCATION

- **Navigating Patient Care & Building the Business**
  - Balancing clinical excellence with business operations: intake, documentation, marketing, and patient retention.

- **DNP vs PhD: What's the Difference & Do You Need It?**
  - A comparison of the Doctor of Nursing Practice (DNP) and Doctor of Philosophy (PhD) paths, helping you decide which is right for your career goals in aesthetics and healthcare.

- **DNP Project Ideas in Aesthetics**
  - Examples of quality improvement, education, and evidence-based projects that align with doctoral competencies.

- **Opportunities for PhD Nurse Scientists**
  - Highlighting potential areas of inquiry and interdisciplinary collaboration for nurses focused on research.

- **Skin of Color in Aesthetic Practice**
  - Gaps in care, lack of representation in clinical trials, and how to advocate for representation in aesthetic medicine.

- **Gaps in Education, Research, and Clinical Training**
  - Why aesthetic curriculum reform is needed, and how nurses can lead the charge.

PART VI: BUSINESS, RESEARCH, AND EDUCATION

- **What's Missing in Marketing: The Cultural Disconnect**
  - Exploring the representation gap in advertising and how inclusive marketing can build trust and drive results.

- **The Pros and Cons of the Aesthetic Industry**
  - An honest discussion about money, mission, burnout, boundaries, and the ethics of selling beauty.

Chapter 30: Navigating Patient Care & Building the Business: Balancing clinical excellence with business operations: intake, documentation, marketing, and patient retention.

We're more than just skilled injectors or laser-savvy clinicians, we are the architects of a full patient experience and the stewards of our aesthetic business success. This chapter bridges the clinical with the operational, helping us create systems that ensure excellence at every stage of care.

Intake: Setting the Standard from the Start

First impressions begin before the first treatment. Our intake process should reflect professionalism, empathy, and attention to detail.

This includes:

- Digital Pre-Visit Forms: Gather medical history, skin concerns, lifestyle factors, and aesthetic goals. Use inclusive, culturally sensitive language.
- Skin Type + Skin Phototype Assessment: Crucial for planning treatments, especially in skin of color.
- Photography Protocols: Baseline photography with consistent lighting and angles is non-negotiable.
- Payment Transparency: Share pricing and packages clearly and professionally.

Documentation & Safety Protocols

Well-documented care builds trust and protects our practice. It also sets the stage for excellent follow-up.

Essential elements include:

- Procedure Notes: Record product, lot numbers, dosage, injection depth, and location.
- Consent Forms: Ensure patients understand risks, downtime, and realistic expectations.
- Post-Treatment Instructions: Provide detailed, written, and verbal guidelines.
- Adverse Event Protocols: Have emergency kits on hand and documented response plans.

Marketing: Building a Brand with Integrity

Marketing isn't vanity, it's visibility. It's how we serve, educate, and build trust in a saturated industry.

- Educational Content: Create blogs, reels, and webinars that highlight your expertise, especially around underserved topics like skin of color or hair loss.
- Representation in Imagery: Use real patients with varied skin tones, ages, and genders. Representation builds credibility.
- Reviews & Testimonials: Encourage honest feedback and highlight patient journeys (with consent).
- Strategic Collaborations: Partner with hairstylists, primary care clinics, or wellness brands for cross-referrals. Think about who else would love to get in front of your audience/clients.

Patient Retention: Relationships > Transactions

The magic is in retention. Loyalty is earned when we make patients feel safe, seen, and supported every time.

- Customized Follow-Up: Schedule routine check-ins post-treatment (and during anniversaries or special milestones).
- Loyalty Programs: Reward patients with value, not just discounts. Think curated skincare kits or priority booking.

- Ongoing Education: Host quarterly "Ask Me Anything" in-person events or webinars for patients. Educated patients are engaged patients.
- Feedback Loops: Ask what they loved and where you could improve. Then, create offers and adjust your practice to address their pain points.

Final Thoughts

Great aesthetic care doesn't stop at clinical expertise, it extends into the business systems that support that care. As nurse practitioners, we're in a unique position to lead with both heart and strategy. When we approach our business like a well-run ecosystem, we don't just thrive, we sustain impact.

31. DNP vs PhD: What's the Difference & Do You Need It?

As a Nurse Practitioner in the aesthetics field, you've likely heard of both the Doctor of Nursing Practice (DNP) and the Doctor of Philosophy (PhD). Both degrees offer high-level opportunities for professional growth, but they're fundamentally different in terms of purpose, focus, and outcomes. Whether you're looking to enhance your clinical expertise or contribute to nursing science through research, understanding the distinctions between these two doctoral paths is crucial in making an informed decision about your future. Let's break it down so you can assess which option aligns best with your aspirations in the world of aesthetics and beyond.

Understanding the DNP: Focus on Clinical Practice
The DNP is a practice-focused doctorate designed to prepare nurses for advanced clinical roles, leadership positions, and healthcare system improvement. It's ideal for those who want to be at the forefront of patient care, translating evidence-based research into real-world clinical practice. DNP-prepared Nurse Practitioners are equipped to take on roles like Chief Nursing Officer, entrepreneur, and innovator, where the emphasis is on improving healthcare outcomes and providing quality, patient-centered care.

For aesthetics, the DNP is highly relevant. If your goal is to understand and operate at the systems level, lead change, and manage a practice or a team, the DNP provides the tools and knowledge needed to excel in systems-level problem solving and operations. With this degree, you'll have the ability to influence healthcare policies, advocate for systemic improvements, and lead innovative approaches in aesthetic treatments, while ensuring high standards of patient safety and satisfaction.

Exploring the PhD: Focus on Research and Education

On the other hand, the PhD is research-oriented and designed for those who generate new knowledge, theories, and practices in nursing and healthcare that help us answer questions for the first time. PhD programs focus heavily on generating research, publishing findings, and advancing nursing science. PhD nurses often work in academic settings, conducting studies, teaching, and mentoring future generations of nurses. This degree also prepares individuals for leadership roles in research-focused institutions or policy-making bodies, where their work can have a significant impact on healthcare practices, education, and patient outcomes.

For those in aesthetics, a PhD is perfect for individuals who are driven by research, eager to explore the latest scientific advancements in aesthetics, or passionate about contributing to evidence-based practices that can shape the future of the field. If you envision yourself pioneering new techniques, conducting groundbreaking research on skin treatments, or owning your own lab, a PhD might be the right path for you!

Key Differences Between DNP and PhD

- Purpose: The DNP focuses on applying research to improve clinical practices and patient outcomes, while the PhD uses research to create new knowledge (this is the type of research most people are familiar with).
- Career Path: DNPs tend to enter clinical or leadership roles within healthcare organizations and businesses, while PhDs often move into academia, research institutions, or policy-making roles.
- Curriculum: DNP programs emphasize evidence-based practice, leadership, policy development, and systems improvement, whereas PhD programs focus on research methodology, data analysis, and theory development. To be clear: today's market requires both DNP and PhD prepared nurses and NPs to understand methodologies and data analysis.

Outcome: DNP graduates are experts in the *application* of research and the advancement of practice; this is what students struggle to understand the most. PhD nurse scientists contribute to the body of knowledge through original research that can shape nursing science, education, and the marketplace.

One example: You want to survey women aged 30-40 about their knowledge of alopecia. In the DNP program, you must find a survey that has already been validated. In the PhD program, you're developing the survey and validating it for clinical practice. This is further complicated by the fact that most students have less than 6 months to collect, with limited time to go through the full IRB review (which is required anytime patients are involved in research to protect their safety). So, many students are encouraged to develop DNP Projects that do not include patients.

Historically, PhD-prepared nurses have developed new knowledge and solutions. However, it typically took an average of 17 years for this information to be applied in clinical practice and benefit patients. The DNP degree was created to reduce this gap. As DNP graduates, we take the new knowledge generated by our PhD colleagues and implement it into various settings, making adjustments as needed based on the availability of resources and desired outcomes.

Some universities require PhD nurse scientists to teach and/or apply for tenure. Outside of these requirements, you need to know that whether you pursue a DNP or PhD as an NP, you can see patients, teach, and conduct research (the type of research may vary).

Another reason universities often prefer PhDs over DNPs for certain academic roles is tied to research-focused positions and the expectation to secure research grants. PhD programs are heavily centered on research methodology, which aligns with many universities' priorities, particularly in the sciences and medical fields, where grant funding is crucial for conducting studies, publishing research, and advancing academic work.

However, it's important to recognize that DNP-prepared nurses and NPS are also fully capable of writing grants. We are trained to lead clinical innovations, integrate research into practice, and improve patient outcomes, skills that are highly valuable in academic roles, particularly those focused on clinical or applied research.

Do You Need a DNP or PhD for Your Aesthetic Practice?

You don't need a DNP or PhD to practice aesthetics or to practice as an NP. There was a call about 20 years ago to require a doctorate and for us to practice at the highest level, primarily to meet the growing demands of the public. While the requirement never became mandated, many schools of nursing have adjusted their programs to include eliminating the baccalaureate program (BSN), creating entry-level master's programs, and offering dual degree programs where NP and DNP degrees are earned simultaneously.

The problem with forcing students to obtain dual degrees, requires students to commit without knowing the expectations, the responsibilities, the purpose, the return (or lack of return) on their investment, and all their options.

Additionally, most of us are not expecting to have to defend our education or respond to all the questions about the lack of standardized nursing education after graduation. As long as you are in the academic bubble, you will only hear positive things about obtaining your doctorate. To better prepare you for the types of questions and criticism that you will hear after graduation, I refer you to documents on the next page.

Google the following documents, as they may be updated regularly.

- The Doctor of Nursing Practice Toolkit
- The American Association of Colleges of Nursing (AACN) Essentials and the Graduate Student - What Does it Mean for Me?
- The State of Doctor of Nursing Practice Education

If you're not intrinsically motivated to obtain a doctorate, if you require other people to validate your commitment to higher education, and if you're not interested in project management, a DNP degree may not be for you. In this case, I'm emphasizing the DNP degree as it's the most controversial, the one most tied to the NP degree, and the one that receives the most questions regarding its utility.

Will You Get Paid More?

No degree can guarantee a specific salary. However, the right skillset (communication, sales, and negotiation), mentorship, research, networking, and confidence can get you anything. Whatever you believe is true. If you don't know how to communicate your value and why you should be compensated for the investment you made in your education, no one else will either. Collectively, as a nursing body, if we continue to accept low pay, we can't blame anyone else but ourselves. Remember, when you sit at the negotiation table, you're not just negotiating for yourself. You're setting the bar for all of us. I encourage you not to make decisions based on fear or with a scarcity mindset. This is especially true in dermatology, where many people are desperate to get their foot in the door, and you're advised to accept just about anything.

As an entrepreneur, keep in mind that you can leverage your intellectual property in ways that can help you earn multiple streams of income outside of your place of employment and beyond the walls of your business. *Remember, plenty of people have done far more with much less.*

DNP annual base salary without benefits or scarcity adjustment (obtained from a consulting firm):
50th percentile - $135K
75th percentile - $158K
90th percentile - $199K
95th percentile - $228K

With benefits and scarcity:
50th percentile - $274K
75th percentile - $322K
90th percentile - $404K
95th percentile - $464K

Which Path is Right for You?

You should know, some DNP graduates return to school to get their PhD because of the type of research they want to conduct, primarily being able to create something from scratch. Additionally, there are dual DNP/PhD (my initial interest) programs and initiatives to encourage DNP-PhD collaborative research. See the **TRAIN Program at Mount Sinai.**

Mount Sinai's Translational Research and Implementation Science for Nurses (TRAIN) Program is a 12-week summer initiative designed to support DNP students from underrepresented or disadvantaged backgrounds. Funded by the NIH's National Heart, Lung, and Blood Institute, TRAIN helps participants become leaders in translating research into clinical practice, with mentorship focused on health disparities, hypertension, and related conditions.

Program Details:

- Program Dates: May - August
- Time Commitment: 30 hours/week
- Eligibility: U.S. citizens or permanent residents enrolled in an accredited DNP program and from NIH-defined underrepresented or disadvantaged groups
- Application Deadline: January
- Benefits: Hands-on research, multidisciplinary education, expert mentorship, and a generous stipend

Application Materials Include:

- CV, personal statement, two recommendations, unofficial transcript, and a signed attestation form from your program leadership.

The decision between a DNP and a PhD ultimately comes down to where you see yourself in the future. Do you want to lead a practice, implement changes in patient care, and improve healthcare delivery in the aesthetics field? The DNP degree may be your best choice.

Do you want to contribute to the scientific understanding of aesthetic practices, shake up the marketplace, conduct research, and influence future education in the field? A PhD may be the right choice.

Both degrees offer incredible potential for growth, but they serve different purposes. The first step is to seek mentorship from both sides, learn how to ask the right questions, and do your own research. Always go back to your WHY.

Final Thoughts

In my opinion, it always behooves a team to have change agents. Change agents are people who understand how to prioritize problems, solve problems with efficiency, establish teams with clear roles and responsibilities, identify early adopters, incentivize buy-in, analyze data, evaluate outcomes, and offer solutions to achieve the objective(s). This is where the DNP graduate can add immense value, but only if they recognize this value, are proactive, and self-driven. If you think about it, these same characteristics could be used to describe entrepreneurs, and you don't need a degree to be an entrepreneur.

Healthcare costs consume the second-largest percentage of the United States' GDP (Gross Domestic Product), yet we have the poorest health outcomes of the high-income countries. The solutions we need are bigger than just focusing on direct patient care. We need systemic and operational-level solutions. NP school alone does not prepare you to solve these problems on a global scale in the digital age, where demographics, science, and technology are changing faster than policy can be passed.

"*At the bachelor's level, they tell you what to think. At the master's level, they want to know what you think. At the doctoral level, you become the they.*" - Kimberly Madison, DNP

Chapter 32: DNP Project Ideas in Aesthetics: Examples of quality improvement, education, and evidence-based projects that align with doctoral competencies.

As DNP professionals, we bring a scholarly lens to clinical problems. The aesthetics industry is ripe for innovation, yet underrepresented in academic literature. This chapter is your springboard for DNP projects that advance practice, promote cultural richness, and demonstrate leadership in a rapidly evolving field.

1. Quality Improvement (QI) Projects

These focus on improving processes or outcomes in your clinical setting.

Improving Documentation Accuracy for Aesthetic Treatments
Aim: Enhance treatment safety and follow-up by introducing standardized charting templates.
Measures: Chart audits, clinician compliance, and patient safety outcomes.

Post-Procedure Care Education for Skin of Color
Aim: Reduce adverse events like hyperpigmentation through culturally tailored post-treatment plans.
Measures: Patient-reported satisfaction, incidence of complications, adherence to protocols.

Reducing No-Show Rates with Automated Reminders and Patient Education
Aim: Increase clinic efficiency by introducing SMS reminders and pre-visit educational videos.
Measures: No-show rates before/after, patient satisfaction, staff workflow efficiency.

2. Evidence-Based Practice (EBP) Projects

These integrate the best available research with clinical expertise and patient preferences.

Best Practices for Treating Melasma in Skin of Color

Aim: Implement a treatment algorithm based on current literature.
Steps: Conduct a literature review, implement a protocol, and evaluate outcomes.
Measures: Patient improvement (via MASI score), satisfaction, and recurrence rates.

Efficacy of Topical Retinoids in Black and Brown Skin

Aim: Assess the tolerability and effectiveness of specific formulations.
Steps: Identify validated educational materials, implement usage protocols, and track outcomes.

Pain Management Protocols for Aesthetic Procedures

Aim: Standardize topical anesthesia and distraction techniques to improve patient comfort.
Measures: Patient satisfaction surveys, procedural completion rates, and reported pain scores.

3. Educational Interventions

These projects often target patients or clinical teams.

Staff Education on Cultural Literacy in Aesthetic Care

Aim: Increase team awareness of racial disparities and skin tone variations in treatment planning.
Tools: Pre/post-training surveys, knowledge assessments, and patient experience feedback.

Patient Education Module: Navigating Injectable Treatments Safely
Aim: Equip patients with accurate, culturally sensitive information about neurotoxins and fillers.
Format: Video + PDF + digital consent.
Outcomes: Patient confidence, informed consent comprehension, and reduced complications.

Developing a CE Course: Laser Safety for Skin of Color
Aim: Deliver evidence-based training to nurse practitioners.
Measures: CE evaluations, participant feedback, and confidence scales.
*Start with the American Nurses Credentialing Center's Nursing Continuing Professional Development Program

4. Policy & Leadership Initiatives
Projects that examine broader systemic impact.

Creating Clinic Policies to Support Inclusive Marketing & Representation
Aim: Ensure that patient-facing materials reflect diverse skin tones and identities.
Measures: Pre- and post-intervention audit, patient perception survey, social media engagement, website analytics, and policy compliance checklist

Building a Nurse-Led Aesthetic Training Curriculum Focused on Culture
Aim: Identify clinical guidelines to implement a scalable curriculum that addresses common gaps in traditional training and orientation programs.
Measures: Pre-/post-course knowledge survey, knowledge retention (4-6 weeks later), completion rates, learner satisfaction score, and track learners' involvement in community events.

Final Thoughts
Whether you're launching your first injectable protocol or redesigning your documentation system, your DNP project is an opportunity to elevate the industry. Don't wait for permission, lead the change. The aesthetic space needs more scholarly voices committed to representation, excellence, and evidence.

See the **Mahogany Dermatology Blog** for more ideas for DNP Projects and entrepreneurs, and the *Dermatology DNP Project Ideas* book available in the **Mahogany Dermatology Shop**.

Inside you'll find:

- Dermatology DNP Project Ideas
- A 2- year roadmap to implementing and disseminating a successful DNP Project
- Aesthetic DNP Project Ideas
- DNP-PhD Collaborative Aesthetic Research Opportunities

Chapter 33: Opportunities for PhD Nurse Scientists: Advancing Aesthetic Science through Research and Collaboration

While the aesthetic industry is often viewed through a clinical or business lens, there is a pressing need for research leadership, especially from nurse scientists with PhDs. As aesthetic care evolves, so must the evidence base that underpins our interventions. PhD-prepared nurses are uniquely positioned to lead this charge, offering rigorous inquiry, critical analysis, and a commitment to improving care for all populations.

Where Nursing Science Meets Aesthetics

The contributions of PhD nurse scientists go far beyond traditional bedside applications. In aesthetic nursing, there are countless unanswered questions related to outcomes, access, ethics, disparities, and product safety, especially in skin of color. From qualitative studies exploring identity and beauty norms to randomized controlled trials on treatment efficacy, the field is a fertile ground for innovation.

PhD-prepared nurses can:

- Design and lead clinical trials that include racially and ethnically diverse populations.
- Investigate long-term outcomes of aesthetic interventions across skin types.
- Examine the psychosocial impact of aesthetic procedures on marginalized communities.
- Develop and validate inclusive assessment tools for aesthetic practice.
- Explore historical and cultural factors influencing patient decision-making and provider bias.

Interdisciplinary Collaboration

To advance aesthetic nursing science, collaboration is key. Nurse researchers can partner with dermatologists, plastic surgeons, sociologists, ethicists, and public health professionals to co-create frameworks that address both clinical excellence and cultural sensitivity. Joint publications, cross-disciplinary research labs, and academic consortia are powerful avenues for this work.

Funding and Institutional Support

Funding agencies like the National Institutes of Health (NIH), Robert Wood Johnson Foundation, and PCORI (funds patient-centered comparative clinical effectiveness research) are increasingly prioritizing balanced opportunities and community-engaged research, making aesthetic-focused proposals more relevant than ever. Topics like representation in clinical trials, access to aesthetic care in underserved areas, or the mental health impact of medical aesthetics are highly fundable when grounded in robust nursing theory and public health relevance.

Institutions also play a vital role. Schools of Nursing can integrate aesthetic research pathways into PhD programs, support dissertation topics in this domain, and foster mentorship pipelines that encourage underrepresented nurse scholars to explore aesthetics as a legitimate and impactful area of study.

The Role of the Aesthetic Community

It's time for the aesthetics community to welcome PhD-prepared nurses not only as clinical experts but as scientists who shape the future of the field. Whether by joining editorial boards, contributing to Think Tanks and Masterminds, speaking at interdisciplinary conferences, or contributing to policy discussions, PhD nurses bring a much-needed lens of inquiry, ethics, and advocacy.

Research Priorities for PhD Nurse Scientists in Aesthetics

- Hair Loss in Middle Eastern and South Asian Populations
  - Study cultural perceptions, prevalence, and treatment outcomes for alopecia and hair transplants.
- Facial Aging and Aesthetic Preferences in Underrepresented Populations
  - Analyze age-related anatomical changes and culturally specific aesthetic ideals in South Asian, Middle Eastern, and African American patients.
- Post-Inflammatory Hyperpigmentation (PIH) Protocols
  - Investigate safe, evidence-based treatment pathways for PIH and melasma, especially in darker skin tones.
- Laser Treatment Safety and Efficacy for Skin of Color
  - Develop laser protocols specific to darker skin tones, particularly for resurfacing and pigmentation correction.
- Clinical Outcomes in SOC Patients Receiving Cosmetic Injectables
  - Examine whether product selection, technique, and post-care recommendations need to be modified for better outcomes.
- Patient Education Tools for Diverse Communities
  - Create culturally sensitive, evidence-informed patient resources for procedures like microneedling, peels, and lasers.
- Access and Belonging in Aesthetic Dermatology
  - Study barriers to entry for SOC patients and propose models to expand safe aesthetic care in underserved communities.
- Cultural Sensitivity in Aesthetic Nursing Practice
  - Evaluate how provider training affects trust, safety, and satisfaction in patients with darker skin tones.
- Provider Knowledge Gaps in Treating Skin of Color
  - Design assessments and interventions to boost provider confidence and decision-making with SOC patients.

- Long-Term Safety and Complications Data in SOC Patients
    - Conduct longitudinal studies to better understand risks and outcomes across diverse populations.
- Clinical Guidelines for the Prevention, Evaluation, and Management of Vascular Occlusion in Patients with Skin of Color: A Delphi Study
    - There is a critical need for evidence-based clinical guidelines to help aesthetic providers prevent, recognize, and manage vascular occlusion in patients with darker skin tones. Current protocols are largely based on visual cues such as blanching and discoloration, which can be delayed or obscured in darker skin tones. This research would use the Delphi method to gather expert consensus from dermatologists, aesthetic NPs, and plastic surgeons who regularly treat skin of color. The outcome would be a standardized, inclusive clinical guide with visual and non-visual assessment criteria, risk-reduction strategies, and tailored treatment algorithms for SOC patients.

Call to Action

For the PhD-prepared nurse reading this: there is space for you here. Your voice is needed to build a research base that reflects real patients, diverse skin types, and culturally aware care. Your work can influence practice, education, and policy in meaningful, measurable ways. Let's reimagine what aesthetic research looks like, led by nurses, informed by justice, and rooted in scientific rigor.

See the **Mahogany Dermatology Blog** for more ideas for PhD nurse scientists and entrepreneurs, and the *Dermatology DNP Project Ideas* book available in the **Mahogany Dermatology Shop**.

Inside you'll find:

- DNP-PhD Collaborative Aesthetic Research Opportunities

Chapter 34: Skin of Color in Aesthetic Practice: Bridging Gaps in Representation, Access, and Evidence-Based Care

The U.S. population is rapidly becoming more diverse, with people of color projected to become the majority by 2045. This demographic shift demands that the aesthetics industry expand its clinical knowledge, cultural awareness, and research base to serve a broader range of skin tones and facial features safely and effectively. Failing to adapt not only widens health disparities but also limits market growth and patient trust in aesthetic providers.

The aesthetic industry has made remarkable advances in recent decades, but the pace of progress has not been evenly distributed. Patients with richly pigmented skin remain underrepresented in clinical trials, underserved in clinical care, and overlooked in marketing and education. As nurse practitioners, we must lead efforts to close these gaps, ensuring that skin of color is not an afterthought but a central priority in aesthetic practice.

Underrepresentation in Research

Despite growing interest in inclusivity, clinical trials for aesthetic products and procedures still skew heavily toward Fitzpatrick skin types I–III. This underrepresentation has significant implications for safety, efficacy, and trust. For example, pigmentary disorders and post-procedure hyperpigmentation are more common in skin of color, yet many protocols are not validated for these populations.

PhD nurse scientists, DNP leaders, and NP educators can:

- Advocate for trial designs that require diverse skin type inclusion when you speak to reps and attend in-person events.
- Collaborate with industry partners to develop and validate protocols tailored to melanated skin.
- Publish case series, reviews, and clinical pearls that highlight best practices for treating patients with skin of color.

Gaps in Clinical Training

Most aesthetic training programs still use light-skinned models and Eurocentric beauty standards as the default. As a result, providers may feel ill-equipped to assess and manage conditions in darker skin tones or, worse, unintentionally cause harm through improper use of devices or treatments.

We must reimagine clinical training to:

- Incorporate culturally aware and clinically accurate instruction on melanated skin.
- Emphasize the nuances of pigment, scar risk, keloid formation, and cultural preferences.
- Use high-quality images, simulations, and models that reflect a range of ethnicities and skin tones.

Patient-Centered Care with Cultural Awareness

Caring for patients of color means more than just knowing how to avoid complications. It requires cultural literacy: an understanding of beauty norms, language, access barriers, and historical mistrust. Many patients have experienced being ignored, stereotyped, or misdiagnosed, especially in dermatologic and aesthetic spaces. We can change that narrative.

Clinical practices can:

- Expand the cultural representation of patient-facing materials, photography, and provider teams.
- Offer intake forms that reflect inclusive language around race, ethnicity, gender, and hair/skin concerns.
- Make time to understand the patient's lived experience and how that informs their aesthetic goals.

Advocating for Systemic Change

Advancing aesthetic representation requires more than one-off trainings or engagement statements. It demands structural change. Nurse practitioners are perfectly positioned to lead initiatives at the policy, academic, and industry levels. Whether through speaking engagements, policy reform, curriculum redesign, or research, we can advocate for sustained change across the board.

A Shared Responsibility

Connectedness in aesthetic care is not a trend, it's a responsibility. Every provider, regardless of background, should be competent and confident in treating skin of color. Every patient, regardless of skin tone, deserves safe, effective, and affirming care. As we grow as clinicians and leaders, let's ensure we're not just expanding our skill sets, but also our reach and our relevance. Let's build an aesthetic landscape where every shade of skin is seen, studied, and served.

Chapter 35: Gaps in Education, Research, and Clinical Training: Why Curriculum Reform in Aesthetics Is Urgent and How Nurses Can Lead It

In aesthetic medicine, the most striking disparities aren't just in clinical outcomes, they're in the curriculum. From foundational education to continuing professional development, there are persistent gaps in what's taught, who's represented, and how knowledge is shared. These oversights have real-world consequences: delayed diagnoses, increased risk of complications, and underprepared providers facing an increasingly diverse patient population.

Nurse practitioners, especially those with advanced degrees, are uniquely positioned to address these challenges not only at the bedside but at the whiteboard, in the research lab, and at the policy table.

Education That Lacks Representation by Design

Many aesthetic training programs rely on outdated models that prioritize Eurocentric beauty norms, fail to include images of melanated skin, and neglect common conditions affecting patients of color. This lack of representation sends a dangerous message: that aesthetics is only for some, and safety protocols don't apply equally to all.

We must:

- Redesign learning materials to include diverse skin tones, cultural norms, and patient goals.
- Integrate topics like pigmentary disorders, hair texture, and cultural literacy into didactic and clinical education.
- Ensure that continuing education offerings are inclusive, research-based, and aligned with modern aesthetic standards.

Research That Leaves Too Many Behind

Aesthetic research continues to suffer from underrepresentation and publication bias. Many studies exclude participants with darker skin tones, and even fewer disaggregate outcomes by race or ethnicity. As a result, much of our clinical decision-making is based on narrow data sets that don't reflect the full spectrum of patient needs.

As nurse scientists and clinical leaders, we can:

- Design and publish inclusive studies.
- Partner with dermatologists, plastic surgeons, and community leaders to co-create protocols for underserved populations.
- Use implementation science to study how training programs affect patient outcomes across racial and ethnic lines.

Clinical Training That Skips the Nuance

Shadowing an injector or learning from a few demonstration videos is not enough, especially when patients expect a high level of safety and personalization. We need structured, competency-based training that includes both technical mastery and cultural awareness.

That means:

- Developing nurse-led training centers with standardized curricula.
- Offering mentorship programs that pair new NPs with clinicians experienced in skin of color care.
- Creating certification tracks or fellowships that emphasize aesthetic inclusivity.

Leadership Starts with Us

When we address these gaps, we don't just improve practice, we advance the profession. Nurses have long been pioneers in patient-centered care, and we have the tools to lead reform in aesthetics as well. Whether we're writing the curriculum, influencing product development, or leading clinical trials, we bring a perspective grounded in culture, empathy, and evidence. This is our moment to shape the future of aesthetics, one that reflects the full beauty and collective richness of the world we serve.

Chapter 36: What's Missing in Marketing: The Cultural Disconnect

In the aesthetic industry, marketing isn't just about promotion, it's a mirror that reflects who we see as beautiful, worthy, and welcome. But too often, that mirror is one-dimensional. It excludes the very audiences we serve, perpetuating a narrow standard of beauty and missing a critical opportunity to connect authentically with today's diverse consumer base.

As nurse practitioners, we sit at the intersection of clinical care and patient trust. When we step into the marketing conversation, we bring a deeper understanding of how representation, or the lack thereof, shapes patient experiences. From website photos to social media reels, every image sends a message. And if that message says "this isn't for you," we risk alienating patients who could benefit most from our care.

The Unspoken Impact of Underrepresentation

Patients from underrepresented backgrounds, especially those with richly pigmented skin, often approach aesthetics with hesitation. They've seen the before-and-after photos that only reflect lighter skin. They've heard the stories of laser burns, botched fillers, or dismissive consultations. When your marketing materials show only one type of skin, one nose shape, or one hair texture, you unintentionally reinforce that exclusion.

This isn't just about culture for culture's sake. It's about safety, access, and trust. Inclusive marketing helps patients feel seen. It builds confidence in your expertise and signals that your practice understands the nuances of treating all skin tones and identities.

Inclusive Marketing as a Clinical Strategy
Representation should be woven into your entire marketing strategy, not tacked on as a one-time campaign.

Ask yourself:

- Do our visuals include people with various skin tones, hair types, facial features, and body shapes?
- Are our educational materials translated or accessible to multilingual audiences?
- Do our testimonials reflect the rich culture of our patient population?
- Are we featuring clinical outcomes in darker skin tones, particularly for pigmentary or texture-based treatments?
- Does our branding align with our mission of culture and excellence in care?

Inclusive marketing begins at intake and extends through every patient touchpoint.

Bridging the Gap with Intention
To move from awareness to action, we need to establish sustainable practices:

- Conduct a Marketing Audit: Review your website, brochures, and digital presence. Who do they reflect? Who is missing?
- Partner with Diverse Creators: Work with photographers, models, and designers who bring fresh perspectives and authentic representation.
- Build Community Relationships: Collaborate with local organizations, influencers, and patient advocates to co-create marketing campaigns that resonate.
- Train Your Team: Ensure everyone understands the value of inclusive language, visuals, and messaging.

This chapter is a call to lead. As nurse entrepreneurs, we have the power to reimagine aesthetics, not just in treatment rooms, but in the cultural narratives we shape. When we prioritize representation, we don't just sell services, we create spaces so people feel like they belong.

Reflection Questions

- Is my current marketing reflective of the community I serve?
- How do I ensure that patients of color feel seen and safe in my clinic?
- Have I unintentionally excluded any identities or skin tones from my materials?
- What stories am I telling with my visuals and language?
- Who is missing from my brand's narrative and why?

Action Steps

Short-Term (0–30 Days):

- Review your website and social media for inclusivity gaps
- Update visual content to include patients with darker skin tones
- Highlight a patient success story that represents a marginalized group

Mid-Term (1–3 Months):

- Collaborate with a diverse photographer or designer for your next shoot
- Add culturally relevant education to your newsletters or posts
- Gather feedback from patients of color on how your brand makes them feel

Long-Term (3–12 Months):

- Create clinic policies around inclusive marketing standards
- Invest in annual cultural sensitivity training for your staff
- Advocate for representation in professional organizations and campaigns

Chapter 37: The Pros and Cons of the Aesthetic Industry

The aesthetic industry is booming, offering unique opportunities for NPs to build rewarding careers. However, with any thriving field comes both advantages and challenges. As we consider entering or expanding in aesthetics, it's important to weigh the pros and cons to make informed decisions that align with both our personal and professional goals.

The Pros

- **High Earning Potential.** One of the most significant draws of the aesthetic industry is the financial opportunity. Procedures such as injectables, laser treatments, and body contouring offer high-profit margins, especially as NPs gain expertise and a loyal patient base. The flexibility to scale services, offer packages, and even launch your own practice means there is substantial earning potential, with many NPs finding it a path to financial independence.

- **Flexible Schedule and Work-Life Balance.** Unlike traditional healthcare settings, the aesthetic field offers the potential for a more flexible work schedule. With the rise of aesthetic practices offering evening or weekend hours, NPs can design their practices to accommodate their personal lives, contributing to better work-life harmony. This flexibility is especially attractive to those who are looking to leave the traditional 9-to-5 routine.

- **Creative and Rewarding Work.** Aesthetics allows NPs to use their clinical skills in creative and visually impactful ways. Helping patients achieve their cosmetic goals and enhance their self-confidence provides both personal satisfaction and professional pride. The instant gratification that comes with seeing the physical results of your work is immensely rewarding.

- **Growing Demand.** As societal attitudes toward beauty evolve, there is a growing acceptance and demand for aesthetic treatments. From Botox® to dermal fillers, patients are increasingly seeking non-invasive options to maintain a youthful appearance. The expanding market, combined with an increasing focus on skin of color, ensures continued growth and opportunity in the field.

- **Potential for Specialization.** Aesthetic medicine offers ample opportunities for specialization. Whether it's focusing on injectables, lasers, or dermatological care, NPs can carve out a niche in areas that align with their interests and expertise. Specializing can elevate your practice, attract specific patient groups, and increase earning potential.

The Cons

- **Initial Investment and Overhead.** Starting or expanding an aesthetic practice requires a significant upfront investment. The cost of equipment, training, and marketing can be prohibitive. Additionally, ongoing expenses like product inventory, rent, and insurance add to the financial pressure. For some, these costs can be a barrier to entry or a challenge when scaling.

- **High Competition.** The aesthetic market is highly competitive, with numerous providers offering similar services. To stand out, NPs must focus on building a strong brand, cultivating patient relationships, and maintaining a high standard of care. Competing with established practices and other practitioners can make it difficult to differentiate yourself in the crowded field. My recommendation? Learn how to leverage your intellectual property.

- **Risk of Burnout.** While aesthetics offers flexible hours, the industry can also lead to burnout. The pressure to keep up with trends, maintain patient satisfaction, and manage the business side of things can be overwhelming. Additionally, the emotional toll of working with patients' self-esteem issues and unrealistic expectations requires strong emotional resilience.

- **Ethical Considerations.** There are ethical challenges inherent in the aesthetic industry. The growing trend of "tweakments" or constant minor procedures can lead to unrealistic beauty standards and patient dissatisfaction. NPs need to navigate these concerns thoughtfully, ensuring that treatments align with patient desires but also prioritize their health and well-being.

- **Regulatory and Legal Concerns.** The aesthetic field is subject to various state and local regulations that govern the scope of practice for NPs. These regulations can vary widely, which makes it essential to stay informed about the legal landscape to avoid overstepping boundaries. Additionally, liability and malpractice risks are present in any medical field, and aesthetics is no exception. Proper insurance and legal protections are necessary.

Checklist: Navigating the Industry with Clarity

- I have a clear mission that guides my clinical and business decisions
- My pricing reflects both value and accessibility
- I maintain boundaries to protect my emotional and mental well-being
- I offer services that align with my ethics, training, and long-term goals
- I assess regularly for signs of burnout and compassion fatigue
- I prioritize patient education over sales or trends
- I stay informed on industry shifts without compromising my core values
- I dedicate time to rest and reflection each week
- My business model is financially sustainable and ethically sound
- I know when to decline opportunities that do not align with my mission

Conclusion

The aesthetic industry offers both opportunities and challenges. As nurse practitioners, we must thoughtfully consider the pros and cons before diving in. While the potential for financial success, professional fulfillment, and flexible work hours is compelling, it's essential to be mindful of the investment, competition, and ethical implications of aesthetic practice. By weighing these factors and making informed decisions, we can build sustainable, impactful careers in aesthetics while maintaining our commitment to patient care and professional integrity.

PART VII: LEGAL, FINANCIAL & PROFESSIONAL GROWTH

- **Business Mentors and Legal Experts You'll Need**
    - Guidance on finding and working with mentors and legal experts to navigate the complexities of running an aesthetic or dermatology practice.

- **Finance, Liability, and Practice Protection**
    - Essential information on financial management, liability coverage, protecting your practice from legal risks, and ethical practice.

- **Resources for Ongoing Learning**
    - A curated list of books and resources that can support your journey as you build a thriving aesthetic or dermatology practice.

- **ChatGPT Prompts, Worksheets & Clinical Templates**
    - Practical tools and prompts to streamline your workflow, from creating SOPs to writing marketing emails and patient documents.

- **Launch Your Skincare Line**
    - Learn how to safely and strategically launch your own skincare line, starting with FDA regulations, cosmetic chemistry, and the clinical standards Nurse Practitioners already know and trust.

PART VII: LEGAL, FINANCIAL & PROFESSIONAL GROWTH

- **Beyond Skincare: 20 Innovative Business Ideas for Aesthetic Nurse Practitioner Entrepreneurs**
    - A curated list of innovative, high-impact business ideas for aesthetic and dermatology nurse practitioners ready to expand their reach, income, and influence beyond traditional services.

38. Business Mentors and Legal Experts You'll Need

As you navigate your career in aesthetics or dermatology, building a strong network of mentors and legal advisors will be key to your success. Running a business isn't just about providing excellent care; it's also about protecting your practice, managing finances, and ensuring compliance with regulations. In this chapter, we'll discuss the importance of business mentors and legal experts in helping you establish and grow your practice.

Why You Need Business Mentors

A business mentor is someone with experience who can provide guidance, advice, and feedback as you make crucial decisions about your aesthetic or dermatology practice. They have likely walked the path you're on and can help you avoid common mistakes, streamline your business strategy, and identify new opportunities for growth.

Here's why a business mentor is crucial:

- Insightful Guidance: Business mentors provide valuable insights based on their own successes and failures. Their experiences will help you avoid pitfalls and accelerate your learning curve.

- Strategic Thinking: As a mentor who has been through the business development process, they can help you think strategically about scaling your practice, marketing your services, and managing day-to-day operations.

- Networking Opportunities: A good mentor will introduce you to key industry contacts, vendors, other professionals, and even potential clients that can enhance your practice.

- Accountability and Support: With a mentor, you're less likely to make critical decisions in isolation. They hold you accountable and are there to support you when things get challenging.

Business Coaches vs Mentors

Business coaches, on the other hand, provide structured, goal-oriented support focused on helping you build a sustainable and profitable business. They work with you to clarify your vision, identify specific business challenges, and create strategic action plans. Their approach is rooted in measurable outcomes, whether it's increasing revenue, improving operations, enhancing team performance, or scaling services, and they typically work within a set time frame to keep you accountable. Unlike mentors, who may offer broad career insights, coaches are hands-on partners in implementing systems and frameworks, refining your business model, and ensuring consistent progress toward your defined goals. It's recommended to have more than one mentor or coach, in and outside of your industry. *See a list of recommendations at the end of this chapter.*

Where to Find Business Mentors & Coaches

- Professional Organizations
    - Tap into nursing, dermatology, aesthetics, and medical spa associations, many offer structured mentorship programs or directories of experienced professionals open to coaching.

- Online Communities & Platforms
    - From Facebook groups to LinkedIn and even platforms like Clubhouse or Mighty Networks, there are thriving communities where aesthetic and healthcare entrepreneurs connect, share advice, and offer mentorship.

- Educational Programs & Masterminds
  - Look for programs designed for nurse entrepreneurs and aesthetic NPs. Many offer built-in coaching or mentorship as part of the curriculum, like incubators, accelerators, or professional masterminds.

- Conferences, Workshops & Networking Events
  - In-person events are goldmines for building mentor relationships. Research the speakers and attendees beforehand. Pro tip: Come with a clear value proposition. Ask smart questions, listen actively, and offer your skills in exchange for their guidance.

- Alumni & Academic Networks
  - Don't overlook your NP school, residency sites, or fellowship programs. Alumni often enjoy paying it forward and can connect you with seasoned mentors or coaches in aesthetics or entrepreneurship.

The Role of Legal Experts

Running an aesthetic or dermatology practice requires adherence to a range of regulations, from patient privacy (HIPAA) to malpractice insurance. Legal experts, including attorneys who specialize in healthcare law, can help ensure that your practice is fully compliant and legally protected.

Here's why legal advisors are indispensable:

- Regulatory Compliance: Laws and regulations change frequently, and healthcare law is complex. Legal experts can guide you on the proper documentation, licensing requirements, and how to maintain compliance with federal and state healthcare regulations.

- Contract Review and Negotiation: You'll likely sign contracts with vendors, suppliers, and other healthcare providers. A legal expert can review contracts and ensure they are favorable and protect your interests.

- Liability Protection: Healthcare professionals, especially those in aesthetic practice, are vulnerable to lawsuits. A legal advisor helps you set up malpractice insurance, drafts waivers, and guides you through the process of managing and mitigating risks.

- Business Structure and Taxes: Lawyers specializing in business law can also help you set up the appropriate legal structure for your practice (LLC, corporation, etc.), helping with liability protection and tax advantages.

Where to Find Legal Experts

- Referrals from Industry Associations: Many professional organizations have a network of legal professionals who specialize in healthcare and aesthetics law.

- Local Bar Associations: Search for lawyers who specialize in healthcare law or small business law in your area. They may offer free consultations to help you determine if their expertise aligns with your needs.

- Online Legal Services: You should seek out attorneys who specialize in healthcare and small business law. I recommend starting with referrals from people in your network and looking up attorneys with legal authority and expertise in your state of practice.

How to Leverage Mentors, Coaches, and Legal Experts Effectively
While mentors, coaches, and legal experts bring significant value, it's important to build a relationship that serves both your personal and professional growth.

Here are a few ways to maximize the impact of their guidance:

- Set Clear Expectations: Be upfront with your mentor, coach, or legal advisor about your goals. Do you need help with scaling your business? Are you navigating a tricky legal matter? Clear communication will ensure that both parties are on the same page.

- Be Open to Feedback: A mentor and coach may provide critical feedback that can be difficult to hear, but it's often necessary for growth. Be open to suggestions and actively listen to their advice.

- Consult Regularly: Schedule regular check-ins with your mentor, coach, and legal expert. Establishing an ongoing relationship will help you stay on track and address any concerns early.

- Respect Their Time: Mentors, coaches, and legal experts are often busy professionals. Come prepared for meetings, be concise in your questions, and be respectful of their time.

Conclusion
Business mentors, coaches, and legal experts are integral to building a successful, sustainable aesthetic or dermatology business. They not only provide essential guidance on growing your business, but also protect you from potential legal pitfalls. Take the time to find the right people to support your journey, and remember that seeking guidance and expert legal advice is a smart investment in the future of your business, now and throughout it's existence.

39. Finance, Liability, and Practice Protection

As a nurse practitioner in aesthetics or dermatology, it's essential to understand the financial and legal aspects of your practice. While clinical skills and patient care are at the core of your work, managing finances effectively, ensuring proper liability coverage, and protecting your practice legally are just as critical. In this chapter, we will explore the financial considerations, liability risks, and strategies to protect your business and career.

Financial Management for Aesthetic Practices
Proper financial management is key to sustaining and growing your practice. While you may have a passion for aesthetics, managing cash flow, expenses, and investments can be overwhelming without a strong financial foundation.

Here are the financial essentials you should consider:
- Setting Up a Financial System: It's imperative to have a clear accounting system in place. This includes tracking income, expenses, and managing patient billing. Software like QuickBooks or Xero can streamline accounting processes and help you manage your finances with ease.
- Understanding Revenue Streams: Aesthetic practices typically have multiple income sources, including consultations, procedures, and product sales. Understand how each revenue stream contributes to your overall income and adjust pricing strategies to reflect demand and costs.
- Expense Management: Aesthetic practices come with high overhead costs, including equipment, supplies, rent, and employee salaries. Regularly review your expenses to ensure you are running as efficiently as possible, and look for areas where you can cut costs without compromising quality.

- Tax Considerations: Proper tax planning is crucial to avoid any surprises at the end of the year. Consult with an accountant familiar with healthcare practices to ensure that you are maximizing deductions, staying compliant with tax laws, and planning for future tax liabilities.
- Setting Financial Goals: Create long-term and short-term financial goals for your practice. Whether it's increasing revenue, expanding services, or paying down debt, financial goals will help you stay focused and measure your practice's progress.

Liability Protection

In the field of aesthetics and dermatology, where patient safety and satisfaction are paramount, liability protection is non-negotiable. Medical professionals face potential legal challenges, ranging from malpractice suits to disputes over services provided. Having comprehensive liability insurance and a strategy to minimize risks is crucial.

- Malpractice Insurance: In today's litigious society, malpractice insurance is essential for protecting yourself against claims of negligence or error. Policies vary based on location, specialty, and coverage limits, so it's important to shop around and find the best option for your practice's needs.
- General Business Insurance: In addition to malpractice insurance, consider getting business liability insurance, which covers various risks, including property damage, injury, and employee-related issues. This is especially important if you have physical locations or employees. Visit the Center for Connected Health Policy to learn about state and national telehealth policies and professional requirements.

- Risk Management Strategies: Implement protocols to reduce your practice's exposure to liability risks. This includes keeping thorough patient records, having clear informed consent forms, following proper sterilization procedures, and regularly reviewing safety guidelines.
- Professional Associations and Legal Support: Join professional organizations that offer legal resources and support for practitioners and/or business owners. They often provide access to legal advice and resources on risk management.

Protecting Your Business Legally

Legal protection for your business goes beyond liability insurance. As a business owner, you'll need to safeguard both the legal and ethical standing of your business.

Consider the following:

- Setting Up the Right Business Structure: The legal structure of your practice (LLC, PLLC, corporation, sole proprietorship) will have implications for liability, taxes, and day-to-day operations. Work with a legal expert to determine the most suitable business structure for your business. The Small Business Administration, your local Secretary of State, and the Chamber of Commerce are great resources to start your research. You can also use ChatGPT to prepare for the conversation and develop a list of topics to discuss, and make the most of your time (especially if the legal expert charges by the hour).
- Compliance with Healthcare Regulations: Compliance with healthcare laws such as HIPAA (Health Insurance Portability and Accountability Act) and state regulations is a must. Ensure your practice's operations, including patient privacy, medical record handling, and consent forms, comply with all applicable laws.

- Employment Law: If you have staff, make sure you understand employment laws and regulations, including payroll, benefits, employee rights, and worker's compensation. Avoid legal issues by adhering to local, state, and federal labor laws.
- Contracts and Agreements: Having well-drafted contracts for employees, vendors, and patients is essential. Consult with a legal professional to ensure that contracts are fair, clear, and legally binding. Having an attorney review all your legal documents before you sign them can prevent disputes down the road.
- Intellectual Property (IP): If you develop unique processes, branding, or intellectual property in your practice, it's important to protect those assets. Consider trademarking your logo, securing copyrights for original materials, and ensuring your brand's name is legally protected.

The Importance of Having a Legal and Financial Team

When building a successful aesthetic practice, you don't have to navigate these financial and legal aspects alone. Surround yourself with a team of experts to guide you through the complexities:

- Financial Advisors: A financial advisor can help you set up retirement plans, manage investments, and provide tax planning. Having a professional who understands healthcare finance is a significant asset.
- Accountants: An accountant who specializes in medical practices can help you manage taxes, optimize deductions, and ensure you stay compliant with tax laws.
- Healthcare Attorneys: A lawyer who specializes in healthcare law can help you with malpractice insurance, regulatory compliance, contract negotiations, and risk management. It's worth investing in legal support to prevent issues before they arise.

- Estate Planning Attorneys: Partner with an estate planning attorney who understands healthcare businesses and aesthetic practices. They can help you structure your assets, protect your business legacy, and create succession plans that align with your long-term financial goals. Proper estate planning ensures your business and your family are secure no matter what the future holds.
- Insurance Brokers: Work with an insurance broker who understands the specific needs of aesthetic practices. They can help you navigate the complex world of liability coverage and choose the right policies for your business.

Financial and legal protections are just as important as the clinical skills you develop throughout your career. Whether you are just starting your practice or looking to expand, understanding how to protect your business financially and legally ensures long-term success and minimizes risks. Having trusted advisors on your team, including financial experts and legal professionals, will provide the support you need to focus on delivering exceptional patient care while safeguarding your practice's future.

Ethics in Aesthetic Nursing: Guardrails for Integrity in Practice

Ethics isn't just about following rules; it's about anchoring your aesthetic nursing practice in integrity, empathy, and sound clinical judgment. In a field where beauty, business, and blurred boundaries often intersect, ethical clarity isn't optional; it's essential.

Why Ethics Matter More Than Ever in Aesthetics

In traditional healthcare settings, ethical frameworks are woven into clinical decision-making. But in aesthetics, where procedures are elective, outcomes are subjective, and social media often dictates demand, aesthetic NPs operate in a space that demands even greater discernment. The decisions we make can influence more than appearance; they can shape self-esteem, identity, and psychological safety.

Ethical aesthetic practice goes beyond obtaining consent or setting pricing. It involves honoring patient autonomy without enabling harmful choices, creating business models that prioritize people over profit, and understanding that our influence, online and in clinic, carries immense weight.

Applying the ANA Code of Ethics in Aesthetic Practice

The American Nurses Association (ANA) Code of Ethics serves as a blueprint for safe, patient-centered care across all settings, including aesthetics. These nine provisions aren't just for hospitals and primary care clinics. They are just as relevant when consulting with a first-time Botox client or designing your social media strategy.

Here's how key provisions show up in our space:

- Provision 1: Practice with compassion and respect, especially when patients come in seeking more than just results.
- Provision 2: Stay committed to the patient's well-being, not your sales goals.
- Provision 3: Protect patient rights and safety, including from procedures that don't serve their best interests.
- Provision 5: Take care of yourself, burnout can be experienced in any setting, and your ethics can erode when you're running on empty.
- Provision 6: Foster an ethical environment in your clinic, on your team, and online.

Common Ethical Dilemmas in Aesthetic Nursing

Ethical issues in aesthetic practice often appear in disguise as marketing decisions, client requests, or business growth strategies.

Examples include:

- Inappropriate patient expectations driven by filtered photos and celebrity culture.
- Requests for off-label treatments without adequate evidence or supervision.
- Body dysmorphia and psychological distress that aesthetic procedures won't resolve.
- Scope-of-practice violations, especially when delegating tasks in med spas.
- Pressure to perform procedures that go against your clinical judgment or values.

Your best tools are going to be setting boundaries, ensuring accurate documentation, and investing in continuous education.

Trauma-Informed, Ethics-Driven Patient Selection
Every aesthetic NP should have a screening process that identifies red flags such as:

- Signs of Body Dysmorphic Disorder (BDD).
- Recent trauma, major life changes, or unstable mental health.
- Patients chasing perfection, not well-being.

It's not unethical to say no, it's unethical not to.

Ethical Practice Is Good Business
When your practice is rooted in ethical standards, everything else flows more sustainably:

- Transparent pricing builds trust.
- Informed consent fosters clarity and safety.
- Patient-centered treatment plans enhance satisfaction and outcomes.
- Clear delegation protocols protect your license and patient safety.

An ethical aesthetic business doesn't just feel better, it performs better. Patients refer, staff stay longer, and your reputation strengthens.

Opportunities for Leadership, Research, and Policy
Aesthetic NPs have a powerful role to play in advancing ethics across the profession. Consider:

- **DNP Projects** exploring trauma-informed aesthetic care, ethical patient selection, or med spa delegation standards.
- **PhD Research** focused on social media's impact on aesthetic self-image and ethical implications.
- **Policy Initiatives** that establish clearer scope-of-practice laws or ethical standards for med spas.
- **Entrepreneurial Models** that center transparency, equity, and inclusivity.

When Ethics Are Compromised: Why Some Aesthetic NPs Are Leaving And What We Must Remember

Some aesthetic Nurse Practitioners are quietly walking away from this specialty, not because they lacked skill, passion, or potential, but because they encountered unethical environments that compromised the core of their nursing identity.

These are NPs who loved aesthetic medicine but found themselves in clinics that prioritized profits over people, where patient safety took a backseat to viral marketing, and where unqualified clinicians and non-medical professionals were given platforms louder than theirs, despite the depth of our education and clinical training. If that's your story, or if you've come close, know you are not alone. Your exit does not define your worth.

Now more than ever, our industry needs nurse leaders who remember who they are. We are nurses first. That title carries not only clinical expertise but a commitment to ethics, advocacy, and excellence. Whether we're injecting filler, educating patients, or mentoring the next generation, the foundations of our practice, the Nursing Code of Ethics, our critical thinking, our trauma-informed care, our understanding of systems, remain our compass.

So, if you're navigating a field that feels unrecognizable or morally murky, return to your roots. Revisit your nursing philosophy. What values brought you into healthcare in the first place? Redefine what success means for you. Is it autonomy? Integrity? Community impact? Let that guide your business or career pivot. Reclaim your voice. You do not need a title, viral reel, or influencer status to be a leader. You lead by how you serve, how you educate, and how you uphold standards in every room you enter.

If you've stepped away from aesthetics and are considering a return, come back stronger, with boundaries, a clear business model, and a mission-driven mindset. Our profession is only as strong as the people brave enough to change it from within. The future of aesthetic nursing needs you. Not just for your technical skill, but for your voice, your vision, and your values.

Final Word: Your Ethics Are Your Edge

In a saturated market, your ethical standards aren't just a compliance requirement, they're a differentiator. They're what help you sleep at night and stand tall in rooms full of influencers, investors, and Instagram filters. As aesthetic NPs, we don't just shape faces. We shape experiences, self-concepts, and safety. Lead with ethics, and everything else, profit, performance, patient loyalty, will follow.

40. Resources for Ongoing Learning

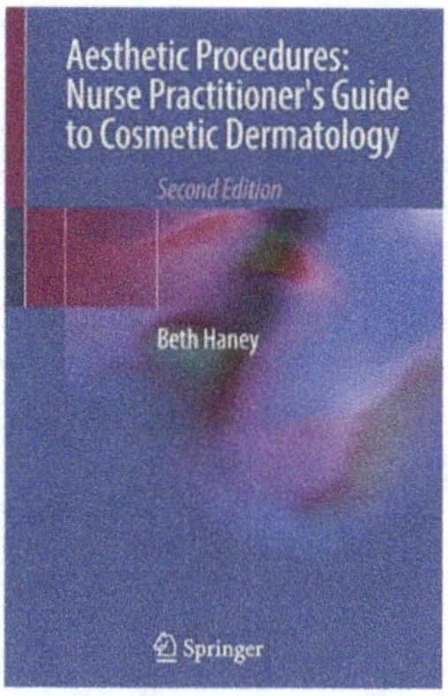

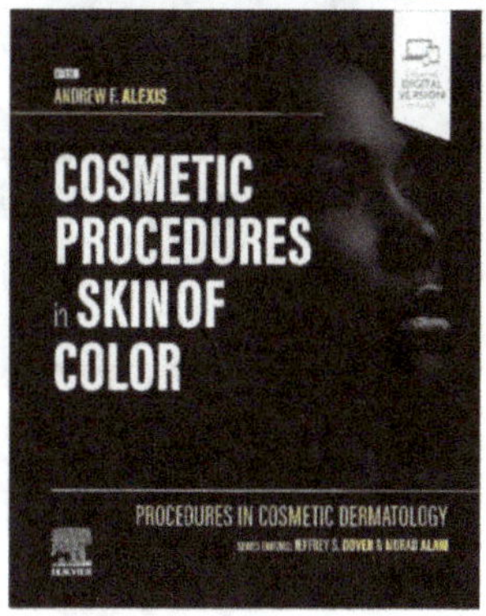

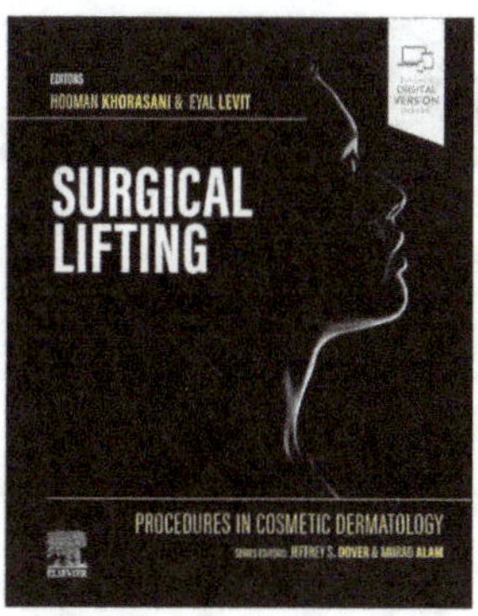

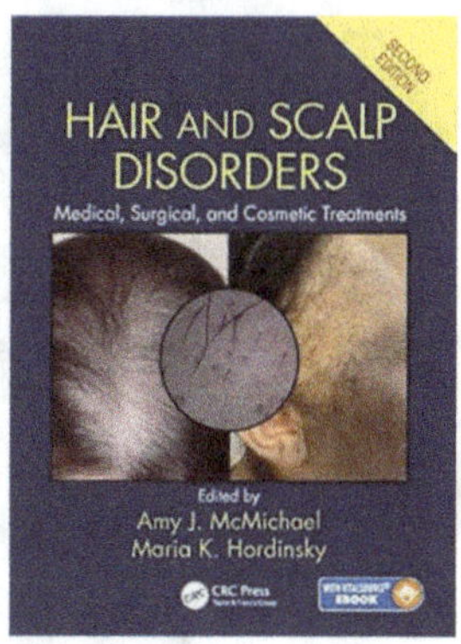

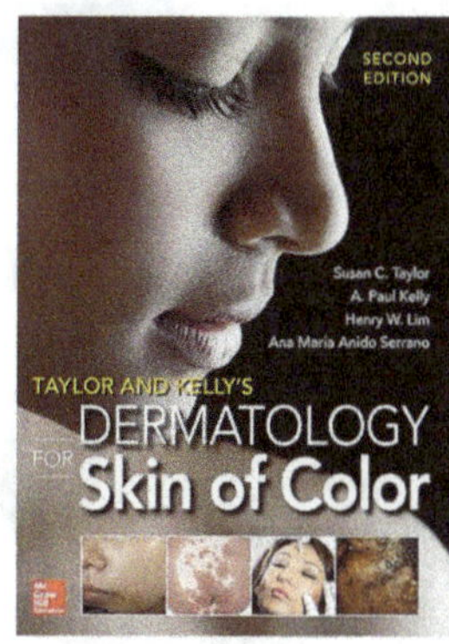

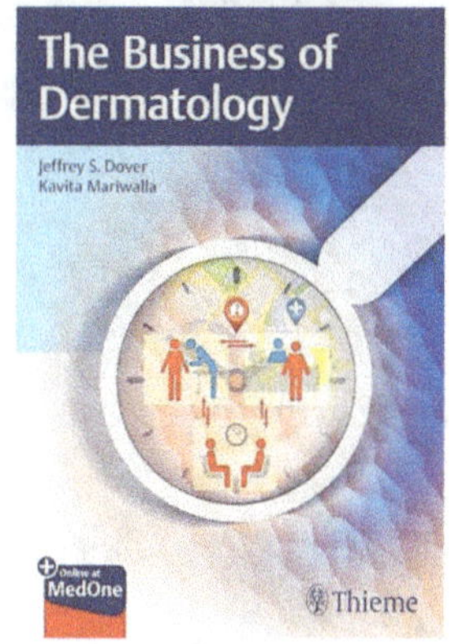

40. Resources for Ongoing Learning: Conferences, Journal, & In-person Training

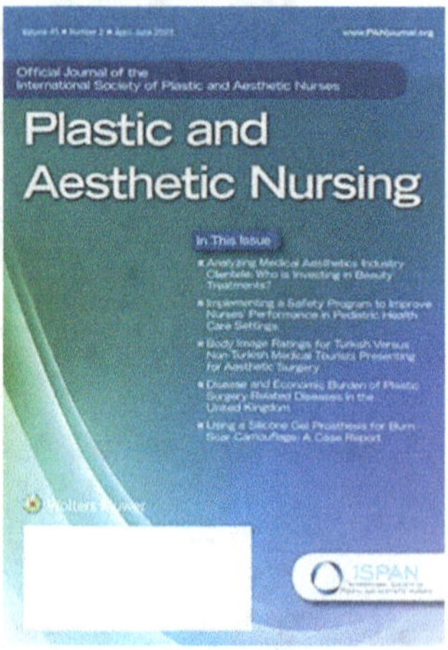

The American Association of Aesthetic Medicine and Surgery

AAOPM
American Academy of Procedural Medicine

JOBSNOB
MEDICAL AESTHETIC JOBS + RESOURCES

SPŌKÉN MEDSPA

Luxe BEAUTY ACADEMY

SKIN CLIQUE

TOP TIER Wellness And Beauty MedSpa

AAFE AMERICAN ACADEMY OF FACIAL ESTHETICS

AUDREY ROSE
Teaching the Art of Beauty
INSTITUTE OF MEDICAL AESTHETICS

GINILLE BEAUTY AESTHETICS

40. Resources for Ongoing Learning: Conferences, Journal, & In-person Training

ISPAN
INTERNATIONAL SOCIETY OF PLASTIC AND AESTHETIC NURSES

SSS SCIENCE OF SKINCARE SUMMIT

SOCIETY OF COSMETIC CHEMISTS
ADVANCING COSMETIC SCIENCE SINCE 1945

AmSpa AMERICAN MED SPA ASSOCIATION

AMERICA'S BEAUTY SHOW

2025 the medical spa show presented by AmSpa

INTERNATIONAL ESTHETICS, COSMETICS & SPA CONFERENCE

The Aesthetic Society

BEAUTYCON

SpaBoss Tribe

WORLD NATURAL HAIR HEALTH AND BEAUTY

THE AESTHETIC SHOW
WHERE SCIENCE MEETS BEAUTY

41. ChatGPT Prompts, Worksheets & Clinical Templates

Time-saving tools and prompt ideas to help you write SOPs, marketing emails, informed consents, and more. In the fast-paced world of aesthetic nursing, systems are our saving grace. While no tool replaces sound clinical judgment, ChatGPT has become one of our favorite assistants for generating first drafts, organizing thoughts, and building repeatable workflows supporting patient care and business growth.

This chapter isn't just about technology, it's about reclaiming your time, refining your processes, and leveraging AI to enhance your expertise (not replace it).

Prompting for Productivity

Here are example prompts:

- Clinical Protocols & SOPs
  - "Draft a standard operating procedure for microneedling with PRP, including pre-treatment, intra-procedure, and post-treatment guidelines."
    - Utilize evidence-based practice guidelines to finalize clinical protocols

- Weekly Team Meeting
  - "Create a 30-minute weekly team agenda with timestamps that includes: things to discuss, action items, feedback, and team appreciation."

- Marketing Emails
  - "Write a 3-part email series to re-engage former patients with a focus on new treatment offerings."

- Social Media Captions
    - "Create 5 educational Instagram captions on hyperpigmentation treatment options for skin of color."
- Patient Education Handouts
    - "Generate a printable aftercare guide for chemical peels tailored to darker skin tones."
- Website Content
    - "Write an FAQ section for a dermatology clinic that specializes in skin of color and inclusive aesthetic care."

Worksheets

Here are additional templates that you can plug into your practice or modify as needed:

- Initial Intake Assessment Template
- Post-Procedure Follow-Up Checklist
- Weekly Content Planning Sheet
- Business Vision & Values Worksheet
- Inclusive Language Review Tool for Marketing

Initial Intake Assessment Template

Prompt:

Create a comprehensive initial intake assessment template for an aesthetic dermatology nurse practitioner clinic. Include sections for medical history, current medications, allergies, Roberts skin type, patient-identified skin and aesthetic concerns, goals of treatment, contraindications, and informed consent. Ensure the template is inclusive of skin of color and gender identity.

Post-Procedure Follow-Up Checklist

Prompt:

Develop a post-procedure follow-up checklist for non-invasive aesthetic treatments such as neuromodulators, dermal fillers, and laser therapies. Include sections for day-of instructions, expected side effects, red flags to report, contact information for urgent concerns, and next steps in the care plan. Address unique considerations for patients with richly pigmented skin.

Monthly Content Planning Sheet

Prompt:

Create a monthly content planning template for an aesthetic nurse practitioner. Include space for daily content across multiple platforms (such as YouTube, LinkedIn, Instagram, email newsletters, and blog posts), content themes, educational topics, promotional goals, marketing strategy, and calls to action. Include optional space for tracking analytics or engagement goals.

Business Vision and Values Worksheet

Prompt:

Design a worksheet that helps aesthetic nurse practitioners define their business vision and core values. Include reflection prompts on mission, long-term goals, brand identity, ideal patient population, and alignment with inclusive care principles. Provide space for both short- and long-term planning.

Inclusive Language Review Tool for Marketing

Prompt:

Generate a checklist to evaluate marketing content in aesthetic nursing for inclusive and culturally sensitive language. Include prompts to assess tone, terminology, imagery, and representation of skin of color, diverse gender identities, and age groups. Offer guidance on avoiding biased language and improving health literacy across materials.

Employee Quarterly Performance Review & Feedback Tool

Prompt:

Create a quarterly performance review template for employees working in an aesthetic practice.

The tool should include:

- Core competencies (e.g., professionalism, patient communication, teamwork, punctuality, skill development)
- Role-specific goals and performance indicators
- A self-reflection section for the employee
- A manager feedback section
- A section for discussing growth opportunities, training needs, and career development
- A feedback loop that allows employees to share their thoughts on team culture, leadership, workflow, and how the NP entrepreneur can better support them
- Ensure the language encourages open, respectful, and future-focused dialogue. Align the tool with values of inclusivity, mentorship, and continuous improvement.

Owner Performance Review Form (Employee Feedback Tool)
Prompt:
Create a respectful, professional, and psychologically safe performance review form that employees can use to provide constructive feedback to the nurse practitioner owner of an aesthetic dermatology practice.

The tool should include:

- Leadership and communication effectiveness
- Support for professional development and growth
- Clarity of expectations, policies, and procedures
- Approachability, conflict resolution, and feedback receptiveness
- Vision alignment and how well the owner models the mission, values, and culture of the practice
- Opportunities for improving team morale, workflow, or inclusion
- An open-ended section for ideas, suggestions, or comments
- Use strengths-based language and design the tool to foster transparency, mutual respect, and team-driven improvement.

Top 100 Workplace Audit & Action Plan

Prompt:

Act as a strategic advisor helping a nurse practitioner entrepreneur evaluate and improve their aesthetic practice to become one of the Top 100 Companies to Work For.

Create a self-assessment and planning worksheet that addresses:

- Company culture, values, and employee engagement
- Leadership transparency, communication, and trust-building
- Compensation, benefits, and work-life balance offerings
- Culture and belonging practices
- Professional development, mentorship, and advancement pathways
- Feedback mechanisms and responsiveness to employee input
- Innovation, collaboration, and recognition systems
- Community involvement and purpose-driven initiatives
- Retention strategies and employee satisfaction metrics

Design the tool to include rating scales, reflection questions, and space for action steps. The goal is to identify areas for celebration and targeted improvement so the NP owner can lead a people-first, high-impact, values-driven company.

Why AI Belongs in Aesthetic Nursing

Think of AI as your creative collaborator, not your clinical compass. It won't replace your expertise, but it can spark ideas, save time, and ensure your messaging and documentation stay consistent and clear.

The real magic happens when you combine your unique voice with systems that scale. When leveraged ethically and thoughtfully, AI can empower aesthetic nurses to lead, educate, and innovate more efficiently than ever before. Always practice ethically when using AI and other digital tools/resources.

42. Launch Your Skincare Line

Starting with Safety: The FDA and Cosmetic Chemistry

Launching your skincare line as an NP is a fantastic opportunity to leverage your clinical expertise while making an impact in the world of dermatology and aesthetics. Unlike other industries, where the product development process may feel foreign or overwhelming, the skills you've honed in patient care can seamlessly translate into the world of skincare creation. The goal is to strategically approach your product launch by starting with the foundational aspects of FDA regulations, understanding cosmetic chemistry, and applying the clinical standards you already know and trust. This will allow you to create a safe, effective, and high-quality skincare line that resonates with your audience and maintains the integrity of your clinical practice.

Understanding FDA Regulations: The Legal Framework for Skincare

As a healthcare professional, the concept of regulations and guidelines is not new to you. The first step in launching a skincare line is to familiarize yourself with the regulatory landscape. In the United States, cosmetics are regulated by the FDA under the Federal Food, Drug, and Cosmetic Act. However, unlike pharmaceuticals, cosmetics do not require pre-market approval by the FDA. What this means is that it’s your responsibility to ensure your products are safe and comply with all necessary regulations before launching them into the market.

For Nurse Practitioners, starting with the FDA’s regulations provides a strong foundation, as it helps set clear boundaries between what is considered a cosmetic versus a drug. For example, a moisturizer that claims to treat eczema is classified as a drug and requires FDA approval, whereas a moisturizer intended for general hydration would be considered a cosmetic. It's crucial to understand these distinctions because they determine your labeling, marketing, and testing requirements.

The FDA also provides guidelines on labeling, ingredient safety, color additives, and claims related to efficacy. As an NP, you already understand the importance of transparency, so using the FDA's guidelines to ensure that your labeling and marketing accurately reflect the benefits of your products will help protect both your brand and your customers. The FDA's guidelines on Good Manufacturing Practices (GMPs) are also invaluable, providing a framework for maintaining consistency and quality across batches. While GMPs are not legally required for cosmetics, following them ensures that your products are manufactured safely and with the highest standards of quality.

Diving into Cosmetic Chemistry: The Foundation of Skincare Formulation

While you don't need to become a full-fledged chemist to launch your skincare line, a basic understanding of cosmetic chemistry is essential for creating safe and effective products. Cosmetic chemistry is the science behind how ingredients interact with the skin, how they are formulated into a product, and how they perform under different conditions. With your background in clinical care, you already have a strong understanding of human biology, which gives you a distinct advantage in skincare formulation.

The first step in cosmetic chemistry is understanding ingredient safety. This includes knowing which ingredients are proven to be safe for different skin types, conditions, and concerns. Some ingredients, like retinoids or acids, can be irritating or contraindicated for certain skin conditions, while others may be highly effective for treating acne, pigmentation, or dryness. Familiarizing yourself with resources like the Environmental Working Group's (EWG) database or the Cosmetic Ingredient Review (CIR) panel will give you insights into the safety profile of different ingredients.

Additionally, understanding the formulation process itself is key. You'll need to learn how ingredients are combined to create stable, effective, and aesthetically pleasing products. Emulsions, preservatives, surfactants, and active ingredients all play a critical role in creating a successful skincare product, and having a basic understanding of how they work together will allow you to make informed decisions when choosing a manufacturer or formulator.

To further ensure the safety and efficacy of your skincare formulations, it's wise to align your ingredient selection with the recommendations of the Cosmetic Ingredient Review (CIR). Established in 1976 by the industry's trade association, originally the Cosmetic, Toiletry, and Fragrance Association and now the Personal Care Products Council, CIR was developed with the support of the U.S. Food and Drug Administration and the Consumer Federation of America. While the Council funds CIR, the Expert Panel for Cosmetic Ingredient Safety operates independently of the cosmetics industry, ensuring unbiased evaluations of ingredient safety. Oversight is provided by a seven-member Steering Committee that includes representatives from the American Academy of Dermatology, the Society of Toxicology, the Consumer Federation of America, industry scientists, and Council leadership.

As an NP entering the skincare space, referencing CIR's peer-reviewed safety assessments provides scientific credibility and enhances consumer trust, positioning your brand as one rooted in integrity, transparency, and clinical excellence.

Good Manufacturing Practices (GMPs): Quality Control from Start to Finish

Good Manufacturing Practices (GMPs) are an essential component of the product development process, ensuring that your skincare line maintains consistent quality across each batch.

GMP guidelines are designed to ensure that cosmetics are produced in a controlled and sterile environment, minimizing the risk of contamination or error. While GMPs are not required by the FDA for cosmetics, they are widely considered a best practice and a sign of professionalism in the industry.

As an NP, you are used to working with evidence-based protocols and patient safety standards. Similarly, GMPs provide a structured framework for maintaining product consistency, ensuring that the active ingredients in your products are accurately dosed and that no harmful contaminants make their way into your formulations. GMPs also ensure proper labeling, packaging, and storage to maintain product integrity throughout its lifecycle.

Clinical Expertise: Applying Patient-Centered Care to Skincare
One of the most powerful advantages you have as a Nurse Practitioner is your deep understanding of clinical care and patient safety. This knowledge can help guide your product development in a way that prioritizes the health and well-being of your customers, just as you would with your patients. Think of your skincare line as an extension of your clinical practice: you offer products that not only meet the needs of your target audience but also align with the clinical standards you uphold in patient care.

To create products that address specific skin concerns, whether it's acne, hyperpigmentation, dry skin, or aging, you can draw from your clinical experience to design targeted solutions that meet the unique needs of your patients. Using evidence-based ingredients and formulations that you know will be both safe and effective will help establish your brand as trustworthy and knowledgeable. You also have the clinical expertise to assess whether the claims made by your skincare line are reasonable, ethical, and backed by solid science.

In addition, you can use your expertise to educate your customers about their skin and the importance of using high-quality skincare products. As NPs, we are often educators, so incorporating patient education into your product branding and marketing can help build trust with your audience and encourage long-term loyalty. Offering transparent information about the benefits and risks of your products, as well as how to use them effectively, will set you apart in a competitive market.

Creating a High-Quality Skincare Line: Combining Regulation, Chemistry, and Clinical Care

By blending your clinical knowledge with an understanding of FDA regulations and cosmetic chemistry, you'll be well on your way to launching a skincare line that is not only effective but also safe, professional, and compliant with industry standards. When you approach your skincare brand with the same level of care, attention to detail, and commitment to patient safety that you bring to your clinical practice, your brand will resonate with consumers looking for products they can trust.

Your deep understanding of dermatology, skin science, and patient care gives you a unique edge in the marketplace, allowing you to create products that address real skincare concerns while adhering to high standards of quality and safety. From ensuring that your formulations are effective and safe to ensuring your products are manufactured in compliance with regulations, you'll set yourself up for success in the skincare industry.

43. Beyond Skincare: 20 Innovative Business Ideas for Aesthetic Nurse Practitioner Entrepreneurs

Skincare is often the most obvious next step, but it's only the beginning. As an Aesthetic NP Entrepreneur, you have the authority, insight, and lived experience to build a business in almost any industry. What matters most is choosing a path that aligns with your expertise, your values, and your lifestyle goals. Below are 20 forward-thinking ideas across clinical innovation, tech, real estate, design, education, and beyond. Each comes with a practical starting point, so you can stop wondering "what's possible?" and start building.

1. Consultant for Skin Tech Startups
Advise companies building diagnostic tools, apps, or wearables to ensure clinical credibility and real-world usability.
Start here: Audit an existing product in the market and write a one-pager on how you'd improve it from an NP's lens.

2. Interior Design Services for Aesthetic Clinics
Help other providers design functional, elevated spaces that enhance both patient experience and workflow.
Start here: Document your own practice design process and offer virtual design consults with a mood board and vendor list.

3. Real Estate Agent Specializing in Medical Spa Builds
Combine your clinical knowledge with real estate licensure to guide aesthetic providers in finding and designing the right space.
Start here: Partner with a broker to shadow transactions, and then niche your marketing toward medical spa owners and start-ups.

4. Brand and Marketing Agency for Aesthetic Entrepreneurs
Create a boutique agency helping aesthetic practices develop a clear brand identity, patient messaging, and high-converting content.
Start here: Offer brand audits and done-with-you content kits to other NPs in your network.

5. Onboarding Specialist for Aesthetic Clinics
Design employee onboarding and training systems that improve retention, reduce legal risk, and protect brand reputation.
Start here: Use your experience to build a customizable onboarding SOP bundle and offer it to new business owners.

6. Equipment Designer for Medical Spas
Design tools that improve safety, ergonomics, or efficiency in the aesthetic treatment space.
Start here: Interview NPs to identify gaps in their workflow, then sketch or prototype a solution with a product designer.

7. Legal Advisor for Health Entrepreneurs
If you hold a legal degree or certification, offer contract reviews, IP protection strategies, or business formation services tailored to NPs.
Start here: Choose one service to specialize in, then build a client funnel through education-based content.

8. Fashion Line for the Modern Aesthetic Pro
Design elevated uniforms, accessories, or loungewear that combine clinical professionalism with style and comfort.
Start here: Survey providers on what they wish existed, then partner with a pattern maker or drop shipping platform.

9. Fellowship or Residency Program Developer
Create a post-graduate training program that upskills aesthetic NPs and helps businesses train staff efficiently.
Start here: Map out a 3-month curriculum based on your onboarding process and pilot it with one mentee or practice.

10. SaaS Founder: Operations or Documentation Tool
Build software that helps NPs track treatment outcomes, manage consent forms, or simplify documentation.
Start here: Outline the user journey and collaborate with a developer to build a no-code MVP (minimum viable product).

11. Strategic Advisor to Device Manufacturers
Provide clinical insights to companies building lasers, injectables, or skin-imaging equipment.
Start here: Create a pitch deck that outlines your expertise and what makes your perspective valuable to R&D teams.

12. Membership-Based Patient Education Platform
Deliver ongoing support, education, and access to care plans through a subscription-based model.
Start here: Record your most commonly taught post-treatment tips and create a digital library for members.

13. Private Label Recovery Kits and Protocols
Bundle curated products and recovery instructions into ready-to-sell kits for post-procedure patients.
Start here: Build partnerships with skincare vendors and test a small batch with loyal patients.

14. Media Company or Podcast Producer for NPs
Launch a content platform that shares stories, clinical pearls, and business advice from within the field.
Start here: Record a pilot podcast episode or write an interview-based blog series on Aesthetic NP journeys.

15. Writer or Author of Clinical and Business Books
Turn your expertise into a publishable asset, whether it's patient-facing guides or NP career playbooks.
Start here: Choose your niche, outline your first three chapters, and write consistently to build momentum.

16. Global Skin Health Consultant
Partner with international health systems or non-governmental organizations (NGOs) to expand education, screening, and treatment accessibility.
Start here: Reach out to global health orgs or university public health departments to explore contract opportunities.

17. Simulation Lab or Virtual Case-Based Education Founder
Build immersive learning tools for graduate students or new grads using real-world cases and digital assessments.
Start here: Convert a real patient case into a simulation script, then partner with a platform to digitize it.

18. Aesthetic Business Incubator for NPs
Create a launch program specifically for NPs starting or scaling aesthetic businesses, from idea to income.
Start here: Repurpose your own journey into a step-by-step roadmap, and test it with a small beta group.

19. Medical Supply Product Line
Develop consumables or reusable tools tailored for NP-owned practices, think sharps containers, treatment carts, or sterile trays. Start here: Survey your peers on what they reorder most, then explore white label or manufacturing partners.

20. Strategic Research Consultant for Startups and Brands
Offer white paper writing, market analysis, or clinical research design to help companies validate or launch aesthetic offerings. Start here: Build a portfolio using your DNP project or prior research, and pitch founders on why evidence builds trust.

BONUS: MARKET ANALYSIS & BUSINESS GROWTH

- **Business Ideation to Creation**
  - Turn your ideas into action with a step-by-step process for developing a business that aligns with your vision, values, and goals in the aesthetics industry.

- **Market Analysis & Projected Profits**
  - Learn how to assess your local market, identify patient needs, and project income streams based on realistic service offerings and pricing strategies.

- **SWOT Analysis**
  - Use this time-tested business tool to assess your strengths, weaknesses, opportunities, and threats, so you can build a resilient and strategic foundation.

- **Business Growth Strategy to Become a CEO**
  - Develop a mindset and action plan to transition from solo provider to CEO, scaling your business through systems, leadership, and sustainable growth.

BONUS: MARKET ANALYSIS & BUSINESS GROWTH

- **AI Chief Financial Officer**
  - Leverage artificial intelligence to manage your finances like a pro, track revenue, forecast expenses, and make data-informed decisions for long-term profitability.

- **Top 20 Questions from Aspiring and Experienced Aesthetic NPs**
  - Honest, insightful answers to the most common questions from NPs at all stages of their aesthetic journey, from starting out to scaling up.

- **How to Connect with Me**
  - Your journey in aesthetics doesn't have to be a solo one. Here's how to stay connected, whether you're seeking mentorship, want to share your success, or need guidance as you grow. You'll find support, resources, and a community ready to cheer you on.

44. Business Ideation to Creation

Turn your ideas into action with a step-by-step process for developing a business that aligns with your vision, values, and goals in the aesthetics industry.

From Passion to Purpose to Profit

Starting your own business in aesthetics isn't just about launching a medical spa or side hustle. It's about creating a practice that reflects your clinical excellence, personal values, and long-term goals. Whether you're passionate about skin of color, wellness-based injectables, or increasing representation in aesthetics, your vision needs structure and strategic direction.

Step 1: Clarify Your "Why"

Before developing your brand or choosing a logo, identify the core reason you're entering aesthetics.

Ask yourself:

- What gap am I addressing in the aesthetics industry?
- What personal or professional experiences are shaping this business idea?
- What impact can I have that will make someone's life easier because my business exists?

ChatGPT prompt:
"Help me refine my business 'why' for an inclusive aesthetics practice targeting [ideal client descriptor]."

Step 2: Define Your Niche

A general approach can make growth difficult in a saturated industry. Defining a specific niche allows you to serve deeply and stand out quickly.

Consider:

- Who do you want to serve?
- What procedures or services do you enjoy most?
- What is your unique differentiator?

Examples of niche aesthetic business ideas:

- Neuromodulators for professional Black women
- Acne and pigment correction boot camps for teens
- Postpartum skincare for new moms
- Mobile toxin parties in high-income areas

ChatGPT prompt:
"List 5 niche business ideas for an NP who specializes in acne and hyperpigmentation in skin of color."

Step 3: Develop a Client-Centered Offer

Your offer should clearly communicate the value of your services and the transformation they provide.

Use this format:
"I help [specific audience] achieve [specific result] through [your method or service]."

Examples:

- I help new moms look refreshed with subtle, 15-minute toxin treatments.
- I help teens manage acne without prescriptions that cause irritation in skin of color.
- I help melanated professionals maintain a youthful glow with skin-safe injectables and professional-grade skincare.

ChatGPT prompt:
"Write 3 client-focused offers for an NP starting an aesthetics side hustle focused on skin of color."

Step 4: Choose the Right Business Model
Start lean and choose a model that supports your lifestyle, budget, and growth plan.

Common business models:

- Solo Suite: Renting a room inside a medical spa or salon
- Concierge: Mobile or in-home services
- Brick-and-Mortar: Opening a full-service clinic or medical spa
- Pop-Up/Events: Offering services through group events or partnerships

ChatGPT prompt:
"Compare solo suite vs. concierge model for a new NP injector with a limited budget."

Step 5: Handle Legal and Compliance Basics
Get the business side in order so you're protected and positioned to grow. At a minimum, plan to:

- Register your business (LLC, PLLC, or other)
- Verify your NP scope of practice and whether a supervising physician is required
- Purchase malpractice insurance that covers injectables and medical aesthetics

- Use HIPAA-compliant intake forms and an EMR system
- Open a separate business bank account
- Set up basic accounting or bookkeeping software

ChatGPT prompt:
"Create a checklist of legal and compliance steps for an NP starting a medical spa in [insert state]."

Step 6: Start Small, Stay Strategic

Avoid the temptation to over invest early. Focus on building credibility, collecting patient results, and refining your systems.

To begin:

- Serve five to ten paying clients or practice models
- Collect before-and-after photos (with permission)
- Create a treatment page with pricing (a simple PDF or landing page is enough)
- Set up an online scheduling system
- Show your process and results consistently on one social platform

ChatGPT prompt:
"Write a first Instagram caption for a new NP injector launching in Houston, TX."

Quick Action Checklist

Use the checklist below to guide your progress from idea to launch:

- Clarified your business mission and niche
- Created a client-focused offer
- Selected your business model
- Completed legal and compliance setup
- Scheduled five practice or model patients
- Set up a basic intake and booking system
- Posted your first public introduction

Final Thoughts

You don't need permission, you need a plan and a community. Your clinical skills, life experience, and personal perspective are all assets. When paired with strategy and consistency, those assets can evolve into a profitable and purpose-driven business that reshapes what leadership in aesthetics looks like.

Chapter 45: Market Analysis & Projected Profits

Learn how to assess your local market, identify patient needs, and project income streams based on realistic service offerings and pricing strategies.

Understanding the Importance of Market Research

Many aesthetic practices fail not because of a lack of skill, but due to poor planning and a lack of understanding about their local, regional, and national market. Market analysis helps you answer key questions about demand, competition, and pricing, which are critical for launching and sustaining a profitable practice.

Step 1: Conduct a Local Competitive Analysis

Start by identifying the aesthetic providers in your area. Pay attention to:

- Services offered (injectables, facials, energy devices, etc.)
- Target audience (age, ethnicity, income level)
- Pricing for key services (Botox, filler, chemical peels, etc.)
- Marketing tactics (social media, influencer partnerships, promotions)
- Brand messaging and unique selling points

Use this to uncover gaps or saturation in your area. Ask:

- What services are underrepresented?
- Who is being left out of current marketing efforts?
- Can I serve a specific group better or differently?

ChatGPT prompt:
"Analyze competitive pricing and patient demographics for medical spas in [your city/state]."

Step 2: Identify Patient Pain Points and Desires

Your ideal patient is more than a demographic. Go deeper to identify:

- What do they wish was different about their skin or appearance?
- What past experiences have they had with skincare or medical spas?
- What thoughts, fears, values, or barriers prevent them from booking treatments?

Gather this data through:

- Peer-reviewed research and industry white papers
- Informal surveys (social media polls, email lists, in-person events)
- Consultations with family, friends, or community members
- Google Trends and patient forums

ChatGPT prompt:

"List 10 common concerns of [ideal client descriptor] seeking aesthetic treatments and how an NP can address them."

Step 3: Determine Service Mix and Pricing

Choose 3–5 core services that align with your clinical skillset, patient needs, and startup budget.

Example service offerings:

- Botox/Xeomin: $11–15 per unit
- Lip filler: $600–800 per syringe
- Chemical peels: $125–250
- Skincare consults + product bundles: $75–150

Avoid undercharging to attract clients. Price according to:

- Product cost and time required
- Your expertise and curated client experience
- The transformation they're going to experience
- The value to the client
- Desired profit margin

ChatGPT prompt:
"Create a starter menu of aesthetic services and fair market pricing for an NP in [city/state]."

Step 4: Project Monthly Revenue Scenarios

Start simple. Project your monthly income based on different scenarios:

Scenario A – Part-Time Injector (10 clients/month)

- 5 Botox clients x $275 = $1,375
- 3 Filler clients x $700 = $2,100
- 2 Skincare clients x $150 = $300
    - Estimated Revenue: $3,775/month

Scenario B – Full-Time Injector (25 clients/month)

- 12 Botox clients x $275 = $3,300
- 8 Filler clients x $700 = $5,600
- 5 Skincare clients x $150 = $750
    - Estimated Revenue: $9,650/month

This is revenue, not profit. You'll subtract product costs, rent, marketing, and taxes to calculate true profit. But these estimates help you plan for cash flow and sustainability.

ChatGPT prompt:
"Estimate gross and net monthly income for an NP injector offering Botox, filler, and peels in a solo suite model."

Step 5: Monitor and Adapt
After launching, continue tracking:

- Booking rates
- Most-requested services
- Referral sources
- Cost per lead (how much you're spending to acquire a client)
- Average revenue per client

This allows you to shift strategy if needed. For example, if chemical peels aren't converting, but your consults are booking at a high rate, you may want to bundle more skincare or add digital products.

Quick Action Checklist

- Researched 3–5 local competitors
- Identified service gaps or underserved groups
- Selected core service mix and initial pricing
- Ran at least two monthly revenue projections
- Established plan to track revenue, costs, and trends

Final Thoughts

Realistic projections lead to intentional growth. You don't need to be the cheapest or busiest injector to succeed—you need to be strategic, data-driven, and willing to adjust. With a firm grasp on your market and numbers, your aesthetics practice becomes not just sustainable, but scalable.

Chapter 45: SWOT Analysis

Use this time-tested business tool to assess your strengths, weaknesses, opportunities, and threats—so you can build a resilient and strategic foundation.

Why a SWOT Analysis Matters

As a nurse practitioner entering aesthetics, you bring unique clinical expertise, but transitioning into entrepreneurship requires a broader view. A SWOT analysis helps you pause and evaluate where you stand—so you can build intentionally, address blind spots, and seize opportunities that align with your long-term vision.

What Is a SWOT Analysis?

SWOT stands for:

- Strengths: Internal advantages you have
- Weaknesses: Internal areas that need development
- Opportunities: External trends or gaps you can leverage
- Threats: External risks or challenges that may affect your success

How to Use the SWOT Framework

Use the grid below as a guide for reflection or team discussion. You can do this quarterly or whenever you're making a big decision (e.g., launching a new service, hiring staff, relocating, etc.).

SWOT Analysis Grid

Strengths	Weaknesses
Clinical expertise in skin health	Limited marketing experience
Strong patient relationships	Minimal startup capital
Passion for aesthetics and outcomes	New to business operations
Ability to educate and empower patients	Need more training on injectables

Opportunities	Threats
Underserved population in your area	High competition from medical spas
Growing demand for natural results	Patient misconceptions about NP-led care
Social media platforms for visibility	Regulatory changes in your state
CE opportunities to expand skills	Rising cost of supplies and rent

ChatGPT prompt:
"Help me complete a SWOT analysis for my new NP-led aesthetics business in [city/state]."

How to Apply Your Insights

Once your SWOT is filled out, ask yourself:

- How can I double down on my strengths?
    - For example, if you're skilled at patient education, consider creating consult guides, webinars, or digital resources that build trust and authority.
- What are quick wins for improving weaknesses?
    - If marketing is a weak area, can you take a short course, hire a consultant, or use AI tools to streamline content creation?
- Which opportunities align best with my goals?
    - You don't have to pursue every opportunity. Focus on the ones that match your niche, passion, and patient needs.

- What threats can I prepare for now?
    - If you anticipate slow months, build a seasonal promotion strategy or diversify your revenue with retail or virtual consults.

Tips for a Strong SWOT

- Be honest. This isn't about perfection, it's about clarity.
- Transparency. It's better to be clear than clever.
- Get feedback. Ask a mentor, colleague, or even a trusted patient to weigh in.
- Revisit often. Your SWOT will evolve as your practice grows.

Quick Action Checklist

- Created your initial SWOT analysis
- Identified at least one action item per quadrant
- Set a reminder to revisit SWOT in 3–6 months
- Used your SWOT to inform pricing, marketing, or service decisions

Final Thoughts

A SWOT analysis is more than a worksheet, it's a mindset. It encourages self-awareness, strategic thinking, and proactive planning. As you build your aesthetic business, keep returning to this tool to stay grounded, focused, and ready for whatever comes next.

46. Business Growth Strategy to Become a CEO

Develop a mindset and action plan to transition from solo provider to CEO, scaling your business through systems, leadership, and sustainable growth.

As aesthetic nurse practitioners, many of us start our journey wearing every hat in the business, from injector to receptionist to marketing strategist. It's an exciting and empowering season, but not one meant to last forever. To scale sustainably, we must transition from being the sole provider to becoming the visionary CEO. That evolution isn't just about growing revenue, it's about building a business that thrives independently of your constant presence.

This chapter is designed to help you shift from task-oriented execution to high-level leadership. The CEO role begins with a mindset. Instead of asking, "What do I need to do today?" we begin asking, "What needs to be true for this business to grow without me doing everything?" It's a shift from short-term hustle to long-term sustainability.

Start by reflecting on how your time is currently spent. Identify the high-leverage activities that only you can perform, those related to growth, innovation, and culture-setting. Everything else can be delegated, automated, or systematized.

Begin documenting your workflows (video recommended and accompany with a narrative that can be AI generated), from patient consultations to inventory management. These standard operating procedures (SOPs) lay the groundwork for training others, maintaining consistency, and freeing up your mental space for strategy.

- If you're looking for a helpful resource to understand systems operations, I recommend the book (available in audio), SYSTEMology by David Jenyns. You'll want to take notes!

As you prepare to build your team, hire with intention. Start small, perhaps with a part-time virtual assistant or clinical support role, but be clear about your expectations, communication methods, and what success looks like in that position. Develop job descriptions that outline duties and performance metrics, and take time to nurture a leadership style that motivates and empowers others rather than micromanages them.

I recommend the 4Es of Employee Engagement, written by Workhuman (a quick Google search will give you access to the PDF):

What do we mean when we talk about "engagement" in the workplace? Quite simply, it's the willingness of an employee to give discretionary effort to a job – to voluntarily do more than the minimum. It's an attitude that manifests itself in behavior.

Financial oversight becomes increasingly important as you grow. Instead of reacting to your bank account balance, begin reviewing key performance indicators monthly, such as revenue per service, patient retention, and net profit margin. Consider working with a bookkeeper or using AI financial tools that act like a "virtual CFO" to help you make data-informed decisions.

Set quarterly and annual financial goals and assess what investments will bring the greatest return: is it in marketing, team development, or expanding service lines?

Vision casting is another hallmark of the CEO role. Set aside time each quarter to zoom out and evaluate your business from a strategic perspective. What's working? What's not? A SWOT analysis can help clarify where to focus your energy (see chapter 44 for guidance). Surround yourself with business mentors, join mastermind groups, and stay anchored in your mission, even as your business model evolves.

As you begin this transition, ask yourself: What would my business look like if I focused solely on growth, innovation, and leadership? What beliefs or fears are keeping me from stepping fully into this role? And how will I define success, not just financially, but personally and professionally?

To support your growth, consider using tools like ChatGPT to streamline your strategy. Try prompts such as: “Draft an SOP for onboarding new aesthetic injectors,” “Create a financial report template for an NP-led medical spa,” or “Write a vision statement for an inclusive, multi-provider aesthetics practice.”

You're not just building a business, you're building a legacy. And that starts with leading like a CEO. Think of a CEO you admire. What can you learn from them in terms of how they run their team, who they have on their team, and how they invest their time?

CEO Planner Page

Designed to help you step into your CEO role with clarity, this planner page supports weekly reflection, goal-setting, and systems thinking.

CEO Weekly Planner Template:

Vision Anchor (Monthly Focus):

What is my North Star for this month?

Top 3 CEO Priorities This Week:

1.
2.
3.

Systems to Build or Refine:

(Think SOPs, automations, and team workflows)

Delegation List:

What will I offload this week to free up my time and mental space?

Team Communication Plan:

When, where, and how will I connect with my team?

Key Performing Indicators (KPIs) to Review (Weekly or Monthly):

- Revenue
- Booked appointments
- Conversion rates
- Patient satisfaction
- Profit and Loss Statements

KPIs are measurable values that show how effectively a person, team, or organization is achieving specific objectives. Think of them as performance checkpoints that help you track progress toward your goals.

Examples:

- In a clinic:
  - Patient wait time
  - Follow-up appointment rate
  - Patient satisfaction score

- For a business:
  - Monthly revenue growth
  - Customer retention rate
  - Website traffic or conversion rate

- For a nurse researcher:
  - Number of participants enrolled in a study
  - Publication or abstract acceptance rate
  - Research milestone completion on time

KPIs help you stay focused on what matters most, evaluate performance objectively, and make data-informed decisions.

CEO Reflection (End of Week):

- What worked well?
- What drained my energy?
- How should I respond to team feedback?
- What did I learn about my leadership style?

47. AI Chief Financial Officer

Leverage artificial intelligence to manage your finances like a pro, track revenue, forecast expenses, and make data-informed decisions for long-term profitability. As a nurse practitioner entrepreneur, you wear many hats. But your role as a financial decision-maker can't be ignored because in aesthetics, every syringe, software subscription, and staff hour affects your bottom line. Fortunately, artificial intelligence can help you step into your role as CFO with more confidence, clarity, and ease.

This isn't about replacing your accountant; it's about augmenting your business brain with smart tools that eliminate guesswork, surface patterns, and reveal where your business is truly thriving (or leaking money).

Smart Budgeting & Expense Tracking

AI-powered platforms like QuickBooks, Found, or Xero now offer predictive insights, not just line-item logging. With bank feed automation, expense categorization, and monthly cash flow snapshots, these tools help you visualize your real-time runway, so you can make decisions before a crisis hits.

Use Case:

You're considering adding a new service like laser. Before you invest in equipment, AI tools can help project revenue potential based on patient demand and volume, and compare it to current treatment profitability.

Forecasting for Growth

AI can analyze seasonality in your bookings, patient preferences, or retail sales and forecast your expected revenue. Whether you're planning your next hire, deciding when to expand, or adjusting your pricing, these tools give you data you can trust.

Try This:

Use an AI-integrated dashboard to simulate different financial scenarios: What happens if you raise prices by 10%? Hire a new team member? Or move to a bigger space? Scenario modeling helps you test ideas without risking your actual business.

Profitability Insights

Many NP entrepreneurs only look at gross income. But AI tools break down what's profitable by tracking the time, cost, and margin of each service. This makes it easier to eliminate what's draining your business, even if it's popular.

Key Questions to Ask Your "AI CFO":

- Which services bring in the most profit per hour?
- When is your business most and least profitable?
- Are your fixed and variable expenses aligned with your growth goals?
- What's your projected cash flow over the next quarter?
- What else should you be considering?

Recommended Tools

- **QuickBooks Online** (with cash flow forecasting and business health score):
    - QuickBooks Online is a go-to for small business bookkeeping, but the real value for aesthetic NPs lies in its cash flow forecasting and business health tools. These features help you visualize incoming and outgoing cash, anticipate slow seasons, and make strategic decisions with confidence.

- **LivePlan** (for budgeting, financial modeling, and pitch planning):
    - LivePlan is perfect if you're seeking funding or planning long-term growth. It allows you to create realistic budgets, model "what-if" financial scenarios, and generate professional pitch decks to share with potential investors or partners.

- **Fathom** (for deeper financial analysis and KPIs):
    - Fathom connects to your accounting software and translates your financial data into meaningful insights. It helps you track KPIs like profit per service or client retention trends, essential for scaling your practice intelligently.

- **Tally or Ramp** (for AI-powered spend management and alerts):
    - These tools use AI to monitor spending, flag unusual charges, and automate expense tracking. For busy NP entrepreneurs juggling clinical and business tasks, they reduce the risk of wasteful spending and increase financial visibility in real-time.

- **Found:**
    - Built specifically for self-employed professionals, Found is a free business banking platform with built-in expense tracking, tax savings tools, and invoicing features. It's ideal for new aesthetic NPs who need an all-in-one, low-maintenance solution to manage money and stay IRS-ready.

- **Xero**:
    - Xero offers a sleek, user-friendly accounting experience with strong bank integrations, real-time financial dashboards, and collaboration features for teams or bookkeepers. It's a great alternative to QuickBooks for aesthetic practices looking for flexibility and ease of use.

Chapter 48: Top 20 Questions from Aspiring and Experienced Aesthetic NPs

Whether you're new to aesthetics or have years of experience behind the needle, questions will always arise. And that's a good thing, questions mean you're thinking critically, staying curious, and wanting to do things right. In this chapter, I've gathered the top 20 questions I hear the most, along with honest, actionable answers. My goal is to help you feel seen, supported, and strategic in your next move.

1. Do I need to take a certification course to start offering aesthetic services?
No, but you do need competency. While there's no national certification required, you are expected to practice within your scope, meet your state's regulatory requirements, and obtain adequate training. A high-quality training course can give you the foundation, but mentorship, hands-on practice, and continuing education are key.

2. What's the best first procedure to offer?
Start with something that's both high-demand and low-risk. Neurotoxin injections (Botox, Dysport, Xeomin) are a solid entry point. They're straightforward to learn, require minimal equipment, and offer great ROI. Build from there based on your comfort, training, and target audience. Invest in more services and goods *after* your clients start asking for them. Consider starting a waitlist and send nurturing emails until you have enough demand (don't make decisions to scale based on emotions or fear of competition). Compare the cost of your investment to your potential revenue from your growing waitlist to identify the right time to launch more services and essentially increase your overhead.

3. Can I start a business if I don't have a collaborating physician?
It depends on your state's practice authority. In full-practice states, you can operate independently. In reduced or restricted practice states, you'll need a collaborating physician. Know your Nurse Practice Act and consult a healthcare attorney familiar with your region.

4. How much money should I save before launching?
You can start lean. Aim for at least $5,000–$10,000 to cover training, insurance, basic supplies, and legal setup. If you're building a medical spa or brick-and-mortar clinic, your startup costs could easily reach six figures. Start with the essentials, then scale intentionally.

5. What kind of insurance do I need?
You'll need malpractice insurance that covers aesthetic procedures (many traditional NP policies exclude aesthetics), general liability, and potentially product liability if you sell skincare or devices. Business insurance is also important. Talk to an insurance broker who specializes in med-aesthetic businesses.

6. What's the best EMR or practice management software for aesthetic NPs?
Look for platforms designed for cash-pay practices. A few popular options include Aesthetic Record, Jane, and Doximity. Choose one that supports scheduling, documentation, before/after photos, inventory management, HIPAA-compliant communication, and marketing integrations.

7. How can I stand out in a saturated market?
By being you. Your background as a Nurse Practitioner, your approach to care, your lived experience, and your story are all branding gold. Get clear on your niche, whether that's men's skincare, skin of color, gender affirming care, injectables for older women, or pregnancy safe treatments and build around it.

8. What procedures can I legally perform as an NP?
This varies by state, collaborating agreement (if required), and facility type. In general, NPs can perform most aesthetic procedures, neuromodulators, dermal fillers, microneedling, lasers, if they've been trained and are operating within scope. Know your laws and document your training.

9. Should I work in aesthetics full time?
Not necessarily, many NPs start part-time while keeping another job for stability. Once your aesthetic income begins to match or exceed your regular salary, you can evaluate whether a full-time transition makes sense for your goals and lifestyle.

10. What's the best way to attract clients without sounding salesy?
Educate, don't sell. Share tips, explain procedures, bust myths, and highlight patient stories. When people trust your expertise, they'll naturally want to work with you. Social media, blogs, and email marketing are your friends.

11. Is it possible to succeed in aesthetics if I'm not an influencer or don't love social media?
Yes! Social media is helpful, but not mandatory. You can build a thriving business through word-of-mouth, community partnerships, email lists, and referral programs. That said, you do need a digital presence. A simple website and an updated Google Business Profile go a long way.

12. How do I price my services fairly and profitably?
Start with your costs, products, time, and overhead, then add your desired profit margin. Benchmark with local competitors, but don't race to the bottom. You're offering expertise and safety, not just a service.

13. What's one thing you wish every aesthetic NP knew?
That you are the asset, not just the products you inject. Your training, ethics, judgment, and ability to build relationships are what make you irreplaceable. Invest in those.

14. How do I avoid burnout while growing my practice?
Design your business around your lifestyle, not the other way around. Incorporate scalable income streams (like digital products or virtual consults), set boundaries with patients, and build a support team. Growth shouldn't come at the cost of your well-being. Join communities with other entrepreneurs in and outside of healthcare.

15. Can I mentor or precept other NPs in aesthetics?
Yes, if you've built experience and have the proper legal protections in place. Mentorship can be a meaningful way to give back and create another income stream. Just be sure to outline clear agreements and responsibilities.

16. What are the most common mistakes new aesthetic NPs make?
Overspending on equipment, undercharging for services, skipping legal/insurance steps, and underestimating how much time marketing takes. Go slow, stay strategic, and always keep learning.

17. How do I talk about skin of color without sounding awkward or unqualified?
With humility and honesty. Acknowledge any gaps in your education, seek out training specific to skin of color, and center the patient's lived experience. Representation matters, and so does preparation.

18. Is it worth getting a DNP or PhD if I want to stay in aesthetics?
Pursuing doctoral studies is a personal choice that costs time and money. If you choose to get a doctorate, there's plenty of work to be done as the industry needs nurse-led scholarship. Your doctoral work can inform practice guidelines, education models, policy, and patient care in aesthetics. See chapter 31 for more details.

19. How can I scale my business without adding more patients to my schedule?
By diversifying your revenue: courses, eBooks, brand partnerships, affiliate marketing, workshops, creating high-ticket offers, and identifying high-ticket clients. Your time is valuable; use your expertise to create assets that work even when you're not.

20. What if I feel impostor syndrome?
Welcome to the club. Every successful NP has felt this way at some point. The key is to take action anyway. Confidence grows from competence and community. Surround yourself with mentors, keep learning, and remind yourself: you belong in this room.

Final Thoughts:
Your questions are valid, and you're not alone in asking them. Keep asking. Keep seeking. Keep building. The aesthetics industry needs more Nurse Practitioners who are committed to advancing evidence-based practice, upholding the highest standards, and lifelong learning.

49. How to Connect with Me

A personal invitation to stay in touch and share your journey into aesthetic nursing and entrepreneurship. Our work is deeply personal. Whether you're a brand-new NP exploring aesthetics or a seasoned clinician scaling your practice, I want you to know you're not navigating this path alone. My journey into dermatology and aesthetics has been enriched by mentorship, collaboration, and community. And I'm committed to paying that forward.

Let's Stay in Touch

You can connect with me in several ways:

- **YouTube:**
  - Subscribe to Kimberly Madison DNP for weekly videos and live Q&As on all things derm, aesthetics, and entrepreneurship.

- **Instagram & LinkedIn**
  - Follow @kimberlymadisondnp (Instagram) and Kimberly Madison, DNP (LinkedIn) for the latest updates in nursing, aesthetics, and entrepreneurship.

- **Website**:
  - Visit mahoganydermatology.com to join the waitlist to be notified about programs, masterclasses, clinical support, in-person meet-ups, free resources, and to shop the Mahogany Dermatology Shop for digital tools and guides.

- **Podcast:**
  - Tune in to TMI: The Melanin Initiative for conversations at the intersection of health literacy, nursing expertise, and entrepreneurship.

- **DMV Dermatology NP + PA Group & DERM NPs + PAs of Atlanta**
  - A networking group for NPs and PAs who practice or aspire to practice in medical, surgical, or cosmetic dermatology. Join us on:
    - Facebook
    - Instagram

- **Email:**
  - Have a question or just want to share your ideas? Email me at hello@mahoganydermatology.com.

APPENDIX

- **You're Hired! 60-90 Day Onboarding & Training Plan**
  - A structured 60-90 day onboarding plan designed to support new aesthetic nurse practitioners in mastering core procedures, understanding clinic operations, and developing business acumen from day one.

- **4-Week Botox Training Roadmap for a New Aesthetic NP**
  - A week-by-week roadmap to help new aesthetic NPs build foundational knowledge, refine injection technique, and gain clinical confidence with botulinum toxin treatments.

- **4-Week Filler Training Roadmap for a New Aesthetic NP**
  - A practical, progressive guide for mastering dermal fillers, covering anatomy, injection safety, patient care, and hands-on technique with both needle and cannula approaches.

- **Botox & Filler Pricing Calculator (Based on Cost per Unit and Time)**
  - A customizable tool to help aesthetic NPs set smart, profitable pricing based on product cost, time spent, and business expenses so you can scale with confidence.

APPENDIX

- **Sample Adverse Event SOP for an NP-Led Medspa**
  - A sample standard operating procedure template for managing adverse events in an aesthetic setting, tailored for nurse practitioner-led practices.

- **SOP Starter Kit for NP-Led Aesthetic Practices**
  - A foundational collection of standard operating procedures designed to streamline clinical care, business operations, and team development for nurse practitioner-led aesthetic practices.

Appendix A:
Aesthetic NP Onboarding & Training Plan (60-90 Days)

Use this to onboard yourself or a new team member to core aesthetic procedures and business operations.

Week 1–2: Orientation & Foundational Training

Goals: Understand practice standards, legal scope, safety, and business model.

- Review Nurse Practice Act and any state aesthetic board regulations
- Complete HIPAA, OSHA, and documentation training
- Understand malpractice policy and patient intake workflow
- Tour of clinic, inventory system, and product handling
- Begin self-study: facial anatomy, toxins/fillers, aging process
- Shadow 3 consultations with emphasis on language and photography

Week 3–4: Skill Building

Goals: Confident with Botox injection zones and safety.

- Injection demo: glabella, frontalis, crow's feet
- Practice on a model under supervision
- Complete competency checklist for botulinum toxin
- Observe 3 post-care visits, note follow-up protocol
- Discuss pricing, follow-ups, and adverse event planning
- Review and practice aspirating technique and emergency drills

Week 5–6: Skill Building

Goals: Understand product selection, planes of injection, and managing risks.

- Injection demo: cheeks, lips, chin
- Assist in cannula vs. needle technique sessions
- Practice reconstitution, drawing, and hygiene protocol
- Emergency training: VO protocol, hyaluronidase dilution
- Chart 3 patients with photos, lot numbers, and technique
- Submit clinical reflection on learning gaps

Week 7–8: Integrated Practice & Business Readiness

Goals: Full consult-to-treatment workflow, patient education, and readiness.

- Perform consult and treatment workflow with supervision
- Present 2 patient cases (assessment → plan → follow-up)
- Review business operations: pricing, policies, reordering supplies
- Develop personal CE plan for the next 6 months
- Meet with supervisor or mentor to review progression
- Complete full competency checklist and sign-off

Reflection

1. Which domain do you feel most confident in? Least confident?
2. How will you maintain your skills if you aren't injecting daily?
3. What is your plan for handling patient dissatisfaction or refund requests?

Appendix B:
4-Week Botox Training Roadmap for Aesthetic Nurse Practitioners

Botox Training Roadmap

Week 1: Foundations of Aesthetic Neuromodulators

Learning Objectives:

☐ Review facial anatomy: muscles of expression, danger zones

☐ Understand botulinum toxin pharmacology and product differences

☐ Know indications, contraindications, and consent processes

Checkpoints:

☐ Can label key facial muscles and explain their function

☐ Can compare Botox, Dysport, Xeomin, and Daxxify

☐ Explains the importance of thorough medical history and consent

Trainer Assessment Questions:
- Walk me through the muscles responsible for glabellar frown lines.
- How do you manage patient expectations around treatment onset and duration?
- What are red flags in a patient history that would make you reconsider treatment?

Week 2: Dosage, Dilution, and Injection Technique

Learning Objectives:

☐ Learn reconstitution techniques and dilution strategies

☐ Practice dosing and injection mapping for upper face (frontalis, glabella, crow's feet)

☐ Demonstrate aseptic technique and patient setup

Checkpoints:

☐ Can reconstitute botulinum toxin correctly and safely

☐ Maps out dosing strategy for a model patient

☐ Demonstrates smooth, confident injection technique under supervision

Trainer Assessment Questions:
- Explain why dilution ratios vary for different treatment areas.
- What landmarks do you use to avoid brow ptosis?
- Show me your injection plan for treating crow's feet.

Week 3: Managing Complications and Patient Follow-Up

Learning Objectives:

- ☐ Identify and manage common side effects and adverse events
- ☐ Learn follow-up protocols and touch-up recommendations
- ☐ Discuss documentation and photography best practices

Checkpoints:

- ☐ Describes steps for handling eyelid ptosis
- ☐ Creates a follow-up and touch-up schedule
- ☐ Completes pre- and post-treatment documentation thoroughly

Trainer Assessment Questions:

- What's your protocol if a patient returns with asymmetric brow elevation?
- Why is documentation especially important in aesthetic practice?
- What are signs of a more serious complication requiring referral?

Week 4: Advanced Case Review and Clinical Integration

Learning Objectives:

- ☐ Review real patient cases and customize treatment plans
- ☐ Evaluate different facial patterns and expressions
- ☐ Simulate full consultations including charting and post-care instructions

Checkpoints:

- ☐ Develops a customized treatment plan for at least 2 cases
- ☐ Confidently leads a mock consultation and procedure
- ☐ Receives final trainer evaluation and readiness assessment

Trainer Assessment Questions:

- Based on this patient's photos, how would you adjust dosing?
- How do you approach treating a hyperdynamic forehead?
- Role play: Walk me through your full patient consultation from start to finish.

Appendix C:
4-Week Filler Training Roadmap for Aesthetic Nurse Practitioners

Dermal Filler Training Roadmap

Week 1: Foundations of Dermal Fillers

Learning Objectives:
□ Understand types of dermal fillers (HA, CaHA, PLLA, PMMA) and their mechanisms
□ Review facial aging and the anatomical layers affected by volume loss
□ Identify danger zones and vascular anatomy critical to injection safety
□ Learn the indications, contraindications, and consent process for filler treatment

Checkpoints:
□ Can differentiate between filler types and explain when to use each
□ Can describe how aging impacts facial volume and contour
□ Can identify high-risk injection zones and describe avoidance strategies
□ Can perform a thorough patient history and discuss informed consent for filler

Trainer Assessment Questions:

- What are the key differences between HA and biostimulatory fillers?
- Describe how midface volume loss contributes to perioral aging.
- How would you educate a patient on potential filler complications and consent?

Week 2: Injection Techniques and Product Selection

Learning Objectives:

□ Learn needle vs. cannula techniques and when to use each
□ Review depth of injection for common treatment areas
□ Practice safety techniques: aspiration, slow injection, product placement
□ Understand filler selection by area (e.g., lips, cheeks, chin, jawline)

Checkpoints:
□ Can demonstrate proper depth of injection for nasolabial folds and cheeks
□ Can explain pros and cons of cannula vs. needle for lower face
□ Can identify ideal filler rheology (G prime, cohesivity) for specific facial zones
□ Can simulate aspiration and post-injection massage techniques on a model

Trainer Assessment Questions:

- What considerations guide your filler selection for lips vs. midface?
- Walk me through your cannula technique for cheek enhancement.

- What strategies do you use to minimize bruising and swelling post-treatment?

Week 3: Managing Complications and Patient Outcomes

Learning Objectives:

□ Understand early vs. delayed filler complications (e.g., Tyndall effect, nodules, occlusion)
□ Learn to identify and respond to vascular compromise
□ Review protocols for filler reversal with hyaluronidase
□ Explore strategies to document and communicate complications clearly with patients

Checkpoints:

□ Can list signs of vascular occlusion and describe immediate steps to take
□ Can prepare and dose hyaluronidase for emergency use
□ Can differentiate between expected side effects and adverse events
□ Can explain follow-up care protocols for post-filler monitoring

Trainer Assessment Questions:

- What are the hallmark signs of vascular occlusion, and how would you respond?
- Describe your process for reconstituting and administering hyaluronidase.
- How do you document and report an adverse filler event?

Week 4: Live Injection Practice and Clinical Confidence

Learning Objectives:

□ Conduct full-face assessment with attention to symmetry, proportion, and patient goals
□ Develop treatment plans based on facial anatomy, filler properties, and safety
□ Perform supervised injections with needle and cannula in low- and high-risk areas
□ Practice patient communication, from consultation through post-treatment follow-up

Checkpoints:

□ Can demonstrate a comprehensive aesthetic assessment
□ Can articulate rationale for selected treatment areas and filler choice
□ Can perform safe, supervised injections in two or more facial zones
□ Can lead a full patient consultation including pre-care, procedure, and aftercare

Trainer Assessment Questions:

- Walk me through your aesthetic analysis of this patient and your treatment plan.
- How do you modify your approach based on patient age, skin quality, or ethnicity?
- What communication techniques help you manage anxious or first-time filler patients?

Appendix D:
Botox & Filler Pricing Calculator: Setting Smart, Profitable Pricing

When it comes to offering Botox and dermal fillers, one of the most critical factors in building a successful aesthetic practice is pricing. It’s not just about covering your product costs; it's about making sure your pricing structure reflects your expertise, the time you invest in each treatment, and the overall health of your business. If we’re being honest, finding that sweet spot between affordability and profitability can be tricky. But with the right approach and the help of a customizable pricing calculator, we can make pricing a strategic, informed decision.

Understanding What Goes Into Your Price

Before we get to the calculator, let's break down the components that influence how we price our Botox and filler treatments. It’s about more than just the cost of the product itself, several factors contribute to your pricing decisions.

- **Cost of Goods Sold (COGS)** – This is the direct cost of the Botox or filler product itself, including shipping and any relevant fees. This number is straightforward but vital. It's easy to forget that every syringe and every unit you inject is a cost that needs to be covered before anything else.

- **Time Spent Per Treatment** – As aesthetic Nurse Practitioners, time is your most valuable asset. The amount of time you spend with each client, from consultation to the actual procedure and any follow-up care, should be reflected in your pricing. While you may charge a flat rate for the procedure itself, time spent is an intangible but crucial factor in delivering quality care.

- **Business Expenses** – Running a profitable aesthetic practice requires more than just the materials and time it takes to perform treatments. There are overhead costs such as rent, utilities, equipment, marketing, insurance, and staff salaries to consider. These expenses should be factored into every price point you set.

- **Desired Profit Margin** – Setting a profit margin is non-negotiable if we are serious about building a sustainable business. The goal isn't just to cover your costs, but to ensure that your pricing allows for growth, development, and the ability to reinvest in your practice. Whether you aim for a modest 20% margin or something more ambitious, your profit margin directly influences the pricing structure.

How the Botox & Filler Pricing Calculator Works

Now that we understand what goes into setting a price, let's talk about the tool itself. A well-designed pricing calculator takes these various elements and simplifies the process, allowing you to set prices that are not only competitive but also sustainable for your business. Here's how we'll approach it:

- **Product Cost per Unit:** The cost of each syringe or vial of product.
- **Treatment Time:** The amount of time it takes to perform the procedure (including consultation and follow-up).
- **Overhead:** A calculated portion of your business expenses (rent, utilities, staff wages, etc.).
- **Desired Profit Margin:** The profit percentage you want to include in each treatment price.

By inputting these numbers into the calculator, we can determine a base price that ensures we're covering our costs and achieving the profitability we need to scale.

Example Calculation

Let's walk through an example:

- Cost of Botox per Unit: $10
- Number of Units per Treatment: 25 units
- Treatment Time per Session: 45 minutes
- Hourly Rate for Your Time: $100 (This is the value you assign to your time spent performing the treatment.)
- Business Expenses Allocation: $50 per treatment (This includes a portion of your monthly overhead costs, divided by the number of treatments you do in a month.)
- Desired Profit Margin: 30%

Now, let's plug these numbers into our calculator:

1. Cost of Goods Sold (COGS) = $10 x 25 units = $250
2. Time Cost = 45 minutes = $75 (since $100/hr = $1.67 per minute, and 45 minutes x $1.67 = $75)
3. Business Expenses = $50
4. Total Cost = $250 (COGS) + $75 (Time) + $50 (Expenses) = $375
5. Profit Margin = $375 x 30% = $112.50
6. Final Price = $375 + $112.50 = $487.50

In this example, the final price for the treatment would be $487.50. This price ensures you're covering all your costs and allowing for a healthy profit margin.

Why This Matters for Your Practice

By utilizing a customizable Botox & Filler Pricing Calculator, we ensure that our pricing decisions are strategic and grounded in our actual costs, time, and expenses. It's about more than just setting a number on the spot, it's about creating a pricing structure that can evolve with your practice as you scale. As you refine your approach, track your costs, and adjust your business strategies, this tool will help you continue to make smart, profitable decisions.

We're not here to just survive in aesthetics; we're here to thrive, scale, and set ourselves up for long-term success. By starting with a solid pricing foundation, we're setting ourselves up to grow with confidence and this calculator is designed to give you an example of what to factor into your pricing.

Appendix E:
Sample Adverse Event Standard Operating Procedure (SOP) for an NP-Led Medical Spa

Purpose:

This SOP outlines the process for managing adverse events in an aesthetic setting, ensuring patient safety and providing clear guidelines for Nurse Practitioners (NPs) and staff. It aims to provide a structured approach to responding to adverse events, documentation, and follow-up care in an aesthetic and dermatological setting.

Scope:

This SOP applies to all Nurse Practitioners, estheticians, and administrative staff working within the medical spa setting. It covers a variety of potential adverse events, including but not limited to allergic reactions, infections, and unexpected outcomes following aesthetic procedures such as Botox, dermal fillers, chemical peels, and laser treatments.

Identification of Adverse Events

Adverse events may occur during or after an aesthetic procedure. These can range from mild to severe and may include, but are not limited to:

- Allergic reactions (rash, swelling, difficulty breathing)
- Infection (redness, warmth, pus, fever)
- Vascular compromise (bruising, hematoma)
- Unsatisfactory aesthetic outcome (over-correction, asymmetry)
- Pain or discomfort (persistent or severe)
- Delayed or unexpected side effects (swelling, numbness, etc.)

Signs and symptoms of an adverse event should be documented immediately.

Immediate Response to Adverse Events

Step 1: Assess the Situation

- Verify the patient's current condition.
- Identify the nature and severity of the adverse event.
- Reassure the patient and provide necessary care based on the clinical findings.

If the situation is severe (e.g., signs of anaphylaxis, significant infection), activate emergency protocols immediately and seek emergency medical assistance.

Step 2: Stabilize the Patient

- Administer appropriate treatment to stabilize the patient based on the adverse event (e.g., administer antihistamines for mild allergic reactions, provide wound care for infections, etc.).
- Ensure that the patient is comfortable and that no further complications arise from the adverse event.

Step 3: Notify the Supervising Physician

- In the case of a severe adverse event, immediately notify the supervising physician or medical director for guidance and further actions, as applicable to your state practice act.

Step 4: Document the Incident

- Ensure that all patient interactions, adverse reactions, and treatments are thoroughly documented in the patient's electronic health record (EHR).
- Document the exact time, nature of the adverse event, steps taken to address the issue, and the patient's response.
- Include the patient’s consent and any photographs as appropriate.

3. Follow-Up Care

Step 1: Schedule Follow-Up Appointment

- For non-severe adverse events, schedule a follow-up visit to ensure the issue is resolving appropriately.
- Provide clear instructions to the patient for monitoring and any required aftercare (e.g., ice packs, medications, etc.).

Step 2: Monitor for Delayed Reactions

- Instruct the patient to monitor for any delayed side effects or complications and report any unusual symptoms immediately.
- Consider follow-up calls to the patient within 48-72 hours after the procedure to ensure no delayed reactions are occurring.

Reporting and Documentation

Step 1: Adverse Event Reporting

- All adverse events, including minor events, should be documented and reported to the appropriate regulatory body (e.g., FDA MedWatch, local health authority).
- For products like Botox or dermal fillers, adverse events should be reported to the manufacturer according to their guidelines.

Step 2: Internal Review and Risk Assessment

- Regularly assess all reported adverse events during team meetings.

- Identify any trends or patterns in adverse events to improve safety protocols and refine treatment protocols.

Step 3: Continuous Education and Training

- Ensure that all staff, including Nurse Practitioners, estheticians, and support staff, receive continuous education on recognizing, preventing, and responding to adverse events.
- Provide regular training on the latest evidence-based best practices for managing adverse events in aesthetic procedures.

Patient Communication and Consent

Step 1: Pre-Treatment Discussion

- Before performing any aesthetic procedure, inform the patient of the possible risks and adverse events associated with the procedure.
- Obtain informed consent that specifically covers potential complications, both common and rare.

Step 2: Post-Treatment Communication

- Upon encountering an adverse event, openly communicate with the patient about the situation.
- Provide the patient with clear information on what steps are being taken to address the issue and explain the possible outcomes.

- Offer emotional support to the patient, acknowledging their concerns while reassuring them that the situation is being handled professionally.

Post-Incident Review

Step 1: Internal Review and Reflection

- Conduct a post-incident review with the team to identify any factors that contributed to the adverse event.
- Discuss potential improvements in pre-treatment assessments, technique, patient education, and protocols.

Step 2: Update Procedures if Necessary

- If the incident reveals any gaps in current procedures or protocols, update them as necessary to prevent recurrence.
- Ensure that any changes to procedures are communicated effectively to the entire team.

Key Points for Adverse Event Management

- Prompt Action: Always act quickly and confidently when an adverse event occurs.
- Clear Documentation: Thoroughly document every step of the process.
- Patient-Centered Care: Prioritize patient safety, satisfaction, and emotional well-being.
- Team Communication: Ensure all team members are informed and on the same page when managing adverse events.

- Continuous Improvement: Use adverse events as learning opportunities to improve practice protocols and safety measures.

Conclusion:

Managing adverse events in an NP-led medical spa is crucial for maintaining patient safety, satisfaction, and the overall success of your aesthetic practice. By implementing a set of SOPs, you will ensure a streamlined approach to handling adverse events, allowing for a professional, effective, and empathetic response to any issues that may arise. The key is in proper training, clear communication, and thorough documentation.

Appendix F:
SOP Starter Kit for NP-Led Aesthetic Practices

1. Clinical Care & Safety Protocols

- Botox & Filler Prep + Injection Room Setup
- Pre-Treatment Patient Education Script
- Post-Treatment Instructions (Print & Digital Templates)
- Adverse Event Escalation Tree
- Emergency Cart Setup & Maintenance SOP
- Photography Standards & Consent Process
- Product Lot Tracking + Adverse Event Linkage

2. Business Admin & Scheduling

- Online Booking System Flow + Manual Override Guide
- Cancelation, No-Show, and Reschedule Policy Workflow
- Intake Form Review + Documentation SOP
- KPI Reporting Frequency & Dashboard Setup
- Supply Forecasting: Monthly Ordering Spreadsheet
- End-of-Day Revenue Reconciliation Process

3. Marketing & Patient Retention

- Monthly Social Media Planning SOP
- Before/After Gallery Posting Policy
- Monthly Email Campaign Template & Workflow
- Referral Program Script + Tracking
- Customer Service Review Request Protocol + Timing Strategy

4. Human Resources & Team Development

- New Hire Onboarding Checklist (Clinical + Admin)
- Role-Specific Competency Checklists
- Weekly Staff Meeting Structure & Notes Template
- Annual Review Prep Packet (For You & For Staff)
- How to Conduct a Clinical Skills Audit
- Confidentiality & Social Media Policy

5. CEO-Level Strategy

- Quarterly Planning Retreat Agenda (Solo or Team)
- Vision + Mission + Values Exercise
- Budgeting & Profit Planning Spreadsheet
- Contractor vs. Employee Matrix
- Expansion Feasibility Checklist
- SOP Update & Version Control Protocol

RESOURCES

Alexis, A. F. (Ed.). (2024). Procedures in Cosmetic Dermatology: Cosmetic Procedures in Skin of Color (1st Ed.). Elsevier.

Amechi, M. & Halpin, J. (2022). Considerations for Laser Therapy, Microneedling, and Chemical Peels When Treating Patients With Skin of Color. *Plastic and Aesthetic Nursing, 43*(1), 14-21. doi: 10.1097/PSN.0000000000000483

Bobonich, M., & Nolen, M. (2018). Competencies for dermatology nurse practitioners. *Journal of the American Association of Nurse Practitioners, 30*(11), 606–613. https://doi.org/10.1097/JXX.0000000000000137

Bobonich, M. A., Nolen, M. E., Honaker, J., & DiRuggiero, D. (2021). Dermatology for Advanced Practice Clinicians: A Comprehensive Guide to Diagnosis and Treatment (2nd Ed.). Lippincott Williams & Wilkins.

Buppert, C. (2023). Nurse Practitioner's Business Practice and Legal Guide (8th Ed.). Jones & Bartlett Learning.

Choi M. S. (2020). Basic rheology of dermal filler. *Archives of Plastic Surgery, 47*(4), 301–304. https://doi.org/10.5999/aps.2020.00731

Haney, B. (2024). Aesthetic Procedures: Nurse Practitioner's Guide to Cosmetic Dermatology (2nd Ed.). Springer International Publishing.

RESOURCES

George, E., Matthews, C., Roche, F., & Taylor. (2023). Beyond the hot comb: Updates in epidemiology, pathogenesis, and treatment of central centrifugal cicatricial alopecia from 2022 to 2021. American Journal of Clinical Dermatology, 24, 81-88. Kelly A, & Taylor S.C., & Lim H.W., & Serrano A(Eds.), Taylor and Kelly's Dermatology for Skin of Color, 2e. McGraw Hill Education.

Kelly A, & Taylor S.C., & Lim H.W., & Serrano A(Eds.), Taylor and Kelly's Dermatology for Skin of Color, 2e. McGraw Hill Education.

Kumarasinghe, P. (2018). Pigmentary Skin Disorders (1st ed.). Springer.

Lee, J. (2020). Multicultural Skin Treatments: Learn How to Effectively Treat Skin of Color by Combining Chemical Peels and Laser Treatments. Retrieved from https://www.joellelee.com/books

Madison, K. (2023). Actionable steps for nurse dreamers. Mahogany Dermatology. Retrieved /news/actionable-steps-for-nurse-dreamers

Madison, K. (2023). Becoming a dermatology nurse practitioner: Credentials and privilege. Mahogany Dermatology. Retrieved /news/becoming-a-dermatology-nurse-practitioner-credentials-and-privileges

RESOURCES

Madison, K. (2023). Becoming a dermatology nurse practitioner: Understanding productivity. Mahogany Dermatology. Retrieved /news/becoming-a-dermatology-nurse-practitioner-understanding-productivity

Madison, K. (2023). Building an inclusive care practice. Mahogany Dermatology. Retrieved /news/building-an-inclusive-care-practice

Madison, K. (2023). Business strategies for the aspiring dermatology nurse practitioner. Mahogany Dermatology. Retrieved /news/business-strategy-for-the-aspiringdermatology-nurse-practitioner

Madison, K. (2023). Cosmetic treatment options for skin of color. Mahogany Dermatology. Retrieved /news/cosmetic-treatment-options-for-skin-of-color

Madison, K. (2023). Legal contracts for nurse practitioners. Mahogany Dermatology. Retrieved /news/legal-contracts-for-nurse-practitioners

Madison, K. (2023). Skin of color resources for parents. Mahogany Dermatology. Retrieved /news/skin-of-color-resources-for-parents

Madison, K. (2024). Access to dermatology education. Mahogany Dermatology. Retrieved /news/access-to-dermatology-education

Madison, K. (2024). Free dermatology resource for nurse practitioners. Mahogany Dermatology. Retrieved /news/free-dermatology-resource-for-nurse-practitioners

RESOURCES

Madison, K. (2024). The importance of learning about skin of color and gender-affirming care in aesthetics training. Mahogany Dermatology. Retrieved https:///news/the-importance-of-learning-about-skin-of-color-and-gender-affirming-care-in-aesthetics-training

Madison, K. (2025). 17 dermatology fellowship and training opportunities for nurse practitioners. Mahogany Dermatology. Retrieved /news/16-dermatology-fellowship-and-training-opportunities-for-nurse-practitioners

Madison, K. (2025). Essential textbook for dermatology in skin of color. Mahogany Dermatology. https:///news/essential-textbooks-for-dermatology-in-skin-of-color

Madison, K. (2025). Hidden dangers: Beauty products, Black women, and the implications for nursing. Mahogany Dermatology. Retrieved /news/hidden-dangers-beauty-products-black-women-and-the-implications-for-nursing-practice

Madison, K. (2025). How Allergan's DREAM initiative is shaping skin of color care for aesthetic and dermatology NPs. Mahogany Dermatology. Retrieved /news/how-allergans-dream-initiative-is-shaping-inclusive-aesthetic-care

RESOURCES

Madison, K. (2025). Improving aesthetics care: Key strategies for dermatology NPs treating skin of color. Mahogany Dermatology. Retrieved /news/improving-aesthetics-care-key-strategies-for-dermatology-nps-treating-skin-of-color

Madison, K. (2025). Leveraging AI and digital innovation opportunities for nurse practitioner entrepreneurs. Mahogany Dermatology. Retrieved /news/leveraging-ai-and-digital-innovation-opportunities-for-nurse-practitioner-entrepreneurs

Madison, K. (2025). Preparing for the AI revolution: A guide for dermatology nursing professionals. Mahogany Dermatology. Retrieved /news/preparing-for-the-ai-revolution-a-guide-for-dermatology-nursing-professionals

Madison, K. (2025). Understanding Fitzpatrick skin type: A critical guide for dermatology nurse practitioners. Mahogany Dermatology. /news/understanding-fitzpatrick-skin-type-a-critical-guide-for-dermatology-nurse-practitioners

Nicol, N. (2016). Dermatologic Nursing Essentials: A Core Curriculum. (3rd Ed.). Lippincott Williams & Wilkins.

Sze Hon C, & Suat Hoon T, & Chee Leok G, & See Ket N(Eds.). (2020). Asian Skin: a Reference Color Atlas of Dermatology and Venereology. (Revised 2nd Ed.). McGraw Hill Education.

RESOURCES

Taylor, S. & Elbuluk, N. (2024). Taylor and Elbuluk's Color Atlas and Synopsis for Skin of Color. (1st ed.). McGraw Hill Education.

Vashi, N. & Maibach, N. (2017). Dermatoanthropology of Ethnic Skin and Hair. Springer.

www.ingramcontent.com/pod-product-compliance
Lightning Source LLC
LaVergne TN
LVHW022200200926
848481LV00006B/1794

* 9 7 9 8 9 8 8 3 5 7 1 4 8 *